Excel
Get the Results You Want

Years 3–4 Opportunity Class Tests

**Sharon Dalgleish,
Tanya Dalgleish, Allyn Jones,
Hamish McLean & Stella Tarakson**

PASCAL
PRESS

Completely new edition incorporating early 2021 Opportunity Class test changes

Reprinted 2024

ISBN 978 1 74125 705 2

Pascal Press Pty Ltd
PO Box 250
Glebe NSW 2037
(02) 9198 1748
www.pascalpress.com.au

Publisher: Vivienne Joannou
Project editor: Mark Dixon
Edited by Mark Dixon and Rosemary Peers
Answers checked by Dale Little and Peter Little
Cover by DiZign Pty Ltd
Typeset by Grizzly Graphics (Leanne Richters)
Printed by Vivar Printing/Green Giant Press

Contents

Introduction .... **i**
    About the test iv
    Reading Test iv
    Mathematical Reasoning Test iv
    Thinking Skills Test iv
    Advice to students v
Sample answer sheets .... **vi**

Sample tests

Reading **1**
Sample Test 1 1
Sample Test 2 8
Sample Test 3 15

Mathematical Reasoning **21**
Sample Test 1 21
Sample Test 2 27
Sample Test 3 32

Thinking Skills **38**
Sample Test 1 38
Sample Test 2 46
Sample Test 3 54

Answers

Reading 61
Mathematical Reasoning 70
Thinking Skills 76

ABOUT THE TEST

The NSW Opportunity Class Placement Test is required for placement in an Opportunity Class in a NSW public school.

These classes offer an extra challenge for academically gifted students with high potential in Years 5 and 6. Selection is based on school results plus the results from the NSW Opportunity Class Placement Test.

Details are available at: https://education.nsw.gov.au/public-schools/ selective-high-schools-and-opportunity- classes/year-5.

The NSW Opportunity Class Placement Test consists of three multiple-choice tests:

- Reading (25 questions in 30 minutes)
- Mathematical Reasoning (35 questions in 40 minutes)
- Thinking Skills (30 questions in 30 minutes).

All answers are marked on a separate answer sheet. This is computer marked.

READING TEST

The NSW Opportunity Class Placement Test includes a Reading comprehension component that asks you to read a number of texts and then answer questions to show how well you understood them.

The question format for the Opportunity Class Placement Test varies from subsection to subsection. At the time of writing, the question format is as follows for the four subsections:

- Literary prose text—multiple-choice questions about one text
- Poetry—multiple-choice questions about one poem
- Factual text—a task which asks you to place sentences or phrases into an information text in a way that makes sense (a cloze task)
- Varied short texts—matching descriptive statements to four short texts on the same theme but with different content and written in different styles or from different perspectives.

MATHEMATICAL REASONING TEST

The NSW Opportunity Class Placement Test includes a Mathematical Reasoning component.

The tests include questions involving Number, Patterns, Measurement, Space, Data, Chance and Working Mathematically. This means you will be familiar with the topics covered in the test but the questions may be more difficult or of a type you may not have seen before.

You will be given some information and asked one question about it. The information may be given in words or might involve a diagram, graph or table. You will be familiar with most question types from classroom work and from other tests you have done, such as the NAPLAN test.

INTRODUCTION

THINKING SKILLS TEST

The NSW Opportunity Class Placement Test includes a Thinking Skills component.

The test includes questions that involve both verbal and non-verbal reasoning skills (critical thinking and problem solving). You may be familiar with the topics covered in the test, although questions might involve something new or unusual.

You will be familiar with some question types from classroom work. Some of the questions will test your understanding of language and grammar; others will test your numeracy skills. The questions may be more difficult or of a type you haven't seen before. You will need to be logical and think carefully about your answers.

ADVICE TO STUDENTS

Each question in the NSW Opportunity Class Placement Test is multiple choice. This means you have to choose the correct answer from either four or five options. You need to read the question in the test booklet then mark your answer on a separate answer sheet.

We have included sample answer sheets in this book—similar to those you will be given in the actual test—for you to practise on.

Under time pressure and test conditions it is possible to miss a question and leave a line on the answer sheet blank. Always check that your answer on the separate answer sheet is written down next to the right number. For instance, check that your answer to question 15 is written down against the number 15 on the answer sheet. There is nothing worse than finding out you have missed a space, especially when time is running short.

Reading answer sheet

Mark your answers here.

To answer each question, fill in the appropriate circle for your chosen answer.

Use a pencil. If you make a mistake or change your mind, erase and try again.

You can make extra copies of this answer sheet to mark your answers to all the Sample Reading tests in this book.

	A B C D		A B C D		A B C D
1	○ ○ ○ ○	9	○ ○ ○ ○	18	○ ○ ○ ○
2	A B C D ○ ○ ○ ○	10	A B C D ○ ○ ○ ○	19	A B C D ○ ○ ○ ○
3	A B C D ○ ○ ○ ○	11	A B C D ○ ○ ○ ○	20	A B C D ○ ○ ○ ○
4	A B C D ○ ○ ○ ○	12	A B C D E F G ○ ○ ○ ○ ○ ○ ○	21	A B C D ○ ○ ○ ○
5	A B C D ○ ○ ○ ○	13	A B C D E F G ○ ○ ○ ○ ○ ○ ○	22	A B C D ○ ○ ○ ○
6	A B C D ○ ○ ○ ○	14	A B C D E F G ○ ○ ○ ○ ○ ○ ○	23	A B C D ○ ○ ○ ○
7	A B C D ○ ○ ○ ○	15	A B C D E F G ○ ○ ○ ○ ○ ○ ○	24	A B C D ○ ○ ○ ○
8	A B C D ○ ○ ○ ○	16	A B C D E F G ○ ○ ○ ○ ○ ○ ○	25	A B C D ○ ○ ○ ○
		17	A B C D E F G ○ ○ ○ ○ ○ ○ ○		

Mathematical Reasoning answer sheet

Mark your answers here.

To answer each question, fill in the appropriate circle for your chosen answer.

Use a pencil. If you make a mistake or change your mind, erase and try again.

You can make extra copies of this answer sheet to mark your answers to all the Sample Mathematical Reasoning tests in this book.

	A B C D E		A B C D E		A B C D E		A B C D E		A B C D E
1	○○○○○	8	○○○○○	15	○○○○○	22	○○○○○	29	○○○○○
2	○○○○○	9	○○○○○	16	○○○○○	23	○○○○○	30	○○○○○
3	○○○○○	10	○○○○○	17	○○○○○	24	○○○○○	31	○○○○○
4	○○○○○	11	○○○○○	18	○○○○○	25	○○○○○	32	○○○○○
5	○○○○○	12	○○○○○	19	○○○○○	26	○○○○○	33	○○○○○
6	○○○○○	13	○○○○○	20	○○○○○	27	○○○○○	34	○○○○○
7	○○○○○	14	○○○○○	21	○○○○○	28	○○○○○	35	○○○○○

Thinking Skills answer sheet

Mark your answers here.

To answer each question, fill in the appropriate circle for your chosen answer.

Use a pencil. If you make a mistake or change your mind, erase and try again.

You can make extra copies of this answer sheet to mark your answers to all the Sample Thinking Skills tests in this book.

	A B C D		A B C D		A B C D
1	○○○○	11	○○○○	21	○○○○
2	○○○○	12	○○○○	22	○○○○
3	○○○○	13	○○○○	23	○○○○
4	○○○○	14	○○○○	24	○○○○
5	○○○○	15	○○○○	25	○○○○
6	○○○○	16	○○○○	26	○○○○
7	○○○○	17	○○○○	27	○○○○
8	○○○○	18	○○○○	28	○○○○
9	○○○○	19	○○○○	29	○○○○
10	○○○○	20	○○○○	30	○○○○

Read the text below then answer the questions.

Alice's Adventures in Wonderland

There was a table set out under a tree in front of the house, and the March Hare and the Hatter were having tea at it: a Dormouse was sitting between them, fast asleep, and the other two were using it as a cushion, resting their elbows on it, and talking over its head. 'Very uncomfortable for the Dormouse,' thought Alice; 'only, as it's asleep, I suppose it doesn't mind.'

The table was a large one, but the three were all crowded together at one corner of it: 'No room! No room!' they cried out when they saw Alice coming. 'There's *plenty* of room!' said Alice indignantly, and she sat down in a large armchair at one end of the table.

'Have some wine,' the March Hare said in an encouraging tone.

Alice looked all round the table, but there was nothing on it but tea. 'I don't see any wine,' she remarked.

'There isn't any,' said the March Hare.

'Then it wasn't very civil of you to offer it,' said Alice angrily.

'It wasn't very civil of you to sit down without being invited,' said the March Hare.

'I didn't know it was *your* table,' said Alice; 'it's laid for a great many more than three.'

'Your hair wants cutting,' said the Hatter. He had been looking at Alice for some time with great curiosity, and this was his first speech.

'You should learn not to make personal remarks,' Alice said with some severity; 'it's very rude.'

The Hatter opened his eyes very wide on hearing this; but all he *said* was, 'Why is a raven like a writing-desk?'

'Come, we shall have some fun now!' thought Alice. 'I'm glad they've begun asking riddles—I believe I can guess that,' she added aloud.

'Do you mean that you think you can find out the answer to it?' said the March Hare.

'Exactly so,' said Alice.

'Then you should say what you mean,' the March Hare went on.

'I do,' Alice hastily replied; 'at least—at least I mean what I say—that's the same thing, you know.'

'Not the same thing a bit!' said the Hatter. 'You might just as well say that 'I see what I eat' is the same thing as 'I eat what I see'!'

[...]

The Hatter was the first to break the silence. 'What day of the month is it?' he said, turning to Alice: he had taken his watch out of his pocket, and was looking at it uneasily, shaking it every now and then, and holding it to his ear.

Alice considered a little, and then said, 'The fourth.'

'Two days wrong!' sighed the Hatter. 'I told you butter wouldn't suit the works!' he added looking angrily at the March Hare.

'It was the *best* butter,' the March Hare meekly replied.

'Yes, but some crumbs must have got in as well,' the Hatter grumbled: 'you shouldn't have put it in with the bread-knife.'

The March Hare took the watch and looked at it gloomily: then he dipped it into his cup of tea, and looked at it again: but he could think of nothing better to say than his first remark, 'It was the *best* butter, you know.'

Alice had been looking over his shoulder with some curiosity. 'What a funny watch!' she remarked. 'It tells the day of the month, and doesn't tell what o'clock it is!'

'Why should it?' muttered the Hatter. 'Does *your* watch tell you what year it is?'

'Of course not,' Alice replied very readily: 'but that's because it stays the same year for such a long time together.'

'Which is just the case with *mine*,' said the Hatter.

Alice felt dreadfully puzzled. The Hatter's remark seemed to have no sort of meaning in it, and yet it was certainly English. 'I don't quite understand you,' she said, as politely as she could.

'The Dormouse is asleep again,' said the Hatter, and he poured a little hot tea upon its nose.

The Dormouse shook its head impatiently, and said, without opening its eyes, 'Of course, of course; just what I was going to remark myself.'

'Have you guessed the riddle yet?' the Hatter said, turning to Alice again.

'No, I give it up,' Alice replied: 'what's the answer?'

'I haven't the slightest idea,' said the Hatter.

'Nor I,' said the March Hare.

Alice sighed wearily. 'I think you might do something better with the time,' she said, 'than waste it in asking riddles that have no answers.'

From *Alice's Adventures in Wonderland* by Lewis Carroll

For questions **1–6**, choose the answer (**A**, **B**, **C** or **D**) which you think best answers the question.

1 The purpose of this text is to
   A educate and inform readers.
   B entertain and amuse readers.
   C warn readers about the dangers of talking to strangers.
   D raise awareness of animal rights.

2 Alice sits at the table because
   A it has been set for many people so she thinks anyone can sit there.
   B the others saw her coming and invited her to join them.
   C she wants to drink a glass of wine with the others.
   D she enjoys solving riddles and wants to join the games.

3 The words 'said with some severity' tell us that Alice
   A doesn't want to get her hair cut.
   B is angry that she hasn't been offered tea.
   C is embarrassed that she sat down without being invited.
   D believes that good manners are very important.

4 The Hatter asked Alice a riddle. The effect of this was to
   A make Alice wish she hadn't sat down.
   B bring the tea party to an abrupt end.
   C change the subject away from the matter of his rudeness.
   D awaken the sleeping Dormouse.

5 In Alice's opinion, the Hatter is
   A friendly and inviting.
   B forgetful and absent-minded.
   C puzzling and difficult to understand.
   D rational and well spoken.

6 The passage contains a watch that shows the date but not the time. This tells us
   A the watch is not working properly because it has been damaged.
   B time is standing still for the duration of this passage.
   C Alice cannot understand what the Hatter is saying.
   D Alice is in an odd fantasy world that differs from the real world.

Read the poem below by Phoebe Cary then answer the questions.

Suppose

Suppose, my little lady,
    Your doll should break her head,
Could you make it whole by crying
    Till your eyes and nose are red?
And wouldn't it be pleasanter
    To treat it as a joke,
And say you're glad 'twas Dolly's,
    And not your head that broke?

Suppose you're dressed for walking,
    And the rain comes pouring down,
Will it clear off any sooner
    Because you scold and frown?
And wouldn't it be nicer
    For you to smile than pout,
And so make sunshine in the house
    When there is none without?

Suppose your task, my little man,
    Is very hard to get,
Will it make it any easier
    For you to sit and fret?
And wouldn't it be wiser
    Than waiting, like a dunce,
To go to work in earnest
    And learn the thing at once?

Suppose that some boys have a horse,
    And some a coach and pair,
Will it tire you less while walking
    To say, 'It isn't fair?'
And wouldn't it be nobler
    To keep your temper sweet,
And in your heart be thankful
    You can walk upon your feet?

And suppose the world don't please you,
    Nor the way some people do,
Do you think the whole creation
    Will be altered just for you?
And isn't it, my boy or girl,
    The wisest, bravest plan,
Whatever comes, or doesn't come,
    To do the best you can?

■ For questions **7–11**, choose the answer (**A**, **B**, **C** or **D**) which you think best answers the question.

7 The title of the poem
    A introduces the poem's key message.
    B indicates it was written a long time ago.
    C suggests the poet wants readers to think carefully.
    D does not suit the poem's content.

8 The poem discusses
    A whether girls and boys should have different toys.
    B the fact that children will eventually grow up.
    C the importance of good manners.
    D the things that can go wrong in life.

9 What do we learn about the children in the poem?
    A They have not learnt to deal with life's disappointments.
    B Their lives have been too easy and as a result they are spoilt.
    C They are ill and physically weak.
    D They are resilient and emotionally well balanced.

10 To 'make sunshine in the house / When there is none without' means to
    A open up the blinds on a gloomy day to let in more sunlight.
    B make an effort to be cheerful despite misfortunes.
    C be grateful that you have a home and family.
    D work hard to obtain a challenging goal and overcome obstacles.

11 The message of the poem is
    A if something can go wrong, it will go wrong.
    B it is better to be safe than sorry.
    C make the best out of what life throws at you.
    D girls and boys should receive equal treatment.

SAMPLE TEST 1

Read the text below then answer the questions.

Six sentences have been removed from the text. Choose from the sentences (**A–G**) the one which fits each gap (**12–17**). There is one extra sentence which you do not need to use.

The Hanging Rock Mystery

In 1967 a book was published whose mystery haunts people to this day. Joan Lindsey's book *Picnic at Hanging Rock* was not only a popular novel, it also became a successful Australian film a few years later. The film is filled with atmospheric panpipe music, giving it an eerie feel. Set in 1900 the story features a group of schoolgirls who live in Appleyard College, a strict boarding house. On Valentine's Day, they set off an excursion to Hanging Rock. **12** _____.

While on the picnic, the schoolgirls and teachers experience some bizarre events. **13** _____. This was at midday, as they settled down for their picnic. After the meal, four of the girls were given permission to go for a walk. As they walked, their manner changed from being happy and carefree to becoming grim and trance-like. Forgetting all warnings about snakes and stinging ants, three of the girls took off their stockings and shoes and began to climb Hanging Rock. They appeared to be hypnotised, which frightened the fourth girl. **14** _____. Hysterical and exhausted, the fourth girl eventually managed to find her way back to the picnic site but the other girls didn't come back. A teacher who went out to look for them also never returned.

A full-scale search was launched by the police for the missing girls. **15** _____. She was unable to explain what had happened but there was something very odd about her. Her clothes and fingernails were torn and bloodied but her bare feet were clean and unscratched. This was puzzling, given that she had been walking barefoot in such a rough environment.

According to both the film and the book, the police were never able to find out what had happened to the missing girls. There was no sign they had been abducted or hurt. Since the film came out, many fans have tried to work out what really happened. **16** _____. Conspiracy theories abound, ranging from avalanches to alien abductions.

The real answer, however, is even stranger. Nothing happened at all! There were no missing girls. The book and film were purely fictional, yet many people were convinced the events had really happened. **17** _____.The author herself even played along, saying she preferred people to make up their own minds. If nothing else, it was a clever way to sell books!

A	For example, all the teachers' watches stop working at the exact same time.
B	They flocked to libraries searching for news articles and police reports.
C	She tried to stop them but was completely ignored.
D	This is a real location, in the Macedon Ranges north of Melbourne.
E	The final chapter of the book that solves the mystery was published after the author's death.
F	This might be because the novel was written as if it were relating historical fact, when in fact it wasn't.
G	One girl was eventually found, unconscious and near to death.

SAMPLE TEST 1

Read the four extracts below on the theme of unusual animals.

For questions **18–25**, choose the answer (**A**, **B**, **C** or **D**) which you think best answers the question.

Which extract …

features an animal that never existed?	**18**	_____
explains why some animal species do not survive?	**19**	_____
provides the most detailed description of an unusual animal?	**20**	_____
describes an animal that is physically impossible?	**21**	_____
contains an intense sense of fear and danger?	**22**	_____
expresses the wonder felt when discovering a genuine new species?	**23**	_____
suggests that people can be overly influenced by popular culture?	**24**	_____
discusses the impact of humans on the animal kingdom?	**25**	_____

EXTRACT A

The moon was shining bright upon the clearing, and there in the centre lay the unhappy maid where she had fallen, dead of fear and of fatigue. But it was not the sight of her body, nor yet was it that of the body of Hugo Baskerville lying near her, which raised the hair upon the heads of these three daredevil roysterers, but it was that, standing over Hugo, and plucking at his throat, there stood a foul thing, a great, black beast, shaped like a hound, yet larger than any hound that ever mortal eye has rested upon. And even as they looked the thing tore the throat out of Hugo Baskerville, on which, as it turned its blazing eyes and dripping jaws upon them, the three shrieked with fear and rode for dear life, still screaming, across the moor. One, it is said, died that very night of what he had seen, and the other two were but broken men for the rest of their days.

From *The Hound of the Baskervilles* by Arthur Conan Doyle

EXTRACT B

It is covered with a very thick, soft, and beaver-like fur, and is of a moderately dark brown above and white underneath. The head is flattish, and rather small than large: the mouth or snout, as before observed, so exactly resembles that of some broad-billed species of duck that it might be mistaken for such […] The tail is flat, furry like the body, rather short, and obtuse, with an almost bifid termination: it is broader at the base, and gradually lessens to the tip, and is about three inches in length: its colour is similar to that of the body. The length of the whole animal from the tip of the beak to that of the tail is thirteen inches. The legs are very short, terminating in a broad web, which on the forefeet extends to a considerable distance between the claws, but on the hind feet reaches no farther than the roots of the claws.

From *The Duck-billed Platypus* by George Shaw, 1798

EXTRACT C

Most snakes slither and slide along the ground, but there are rumours of snakes that travel by rolling around like wheels! They supposedly grip their tails in their mouths and roll after their prey at great speeds. On reaching their unfortunate victims, the snakes unroll themselves and strike their prey down with stingers that are found on their tails.

Known as hoop snakes, zoologists dispute the existence of these bizarre creatures. They point out that rolling is an unnatural way for snakes to travel: their muscles and bones simply are not made that way.

Yet sightings of hoop snakes have been made across the United States and even here in Australia. Countless eyewitnesses have come forward; however, they have not been able to offer any physical proof. Perhaps many of the sightings were influenced by a series of stories written about a cowboy called Pecos Bill, who fought off the deadly hoop snakes. Even so, the question remains: What inspired the author to write about these creatures? Sightings of hoop snakes actually predate the stories. So did the creatures come from the writer's imagination or somewhere else?

EXTRACT D

The Tasmanian Tiger, also known as the thylacine, is generally considered to be extinct. Thylacines looked like a cross between a dog and a kangaroo. They walked on four legs with dog-like bodies but had heavy stiff tails like kangaroos. They were brownish grey with long tiger stripes along their backs.

Nobody is completely sure why they became extinct but it is most likely due to a combination of factors. It is possible that dingoes were partly to blame, as they outcompeted thylacines for food and habitat. Climate change also seems to have had an impact on the thylacine's habitat, further weakening the species. Hunting was definitely a problem, as many farmers slaughtered the wild animals, who they blamed for killing livestock. By the time people realised the species was endangered, it was too late to save them.

It is thought that thylacines died out in mainland Australia around 3000 years ago. Since colonisation, they could only be found in Tasmania, where the last known thylacine died in 1936. This hasn't stopped many people from claiming to have spotted them, however. Sightings have been made throughout the country, in habitat that would indeed suit the thylacines. It's possible that some may have survived and the species might one day be officially rediscovered.

SAMPLE TEST 2

Read the text below and answer the questions.

Here Comes Hercules

(Tim accidentally breaks an Ancient Greek vase and Hercules, the hero from mythology, emerges. He has been trapped since ancient days, and vows to help the boy who allowed him to escape.)

Tim gripped the tiger-skin rug with both hands and heaved. He dragged it down the hall and out the back door. Getting it onto the clothesline took all his strength. He pulled and tugged and hauled. Finally, the stuffed head flopped over the line.

'Don't worry, this won't hurt a bit,' Tim said. 'Soon have you good as new.' He fastened some pegs on the tiger's fur to stop it from sliding off. He shook it. A cloud of dust flew out, making him sneeze. He needed something to hit the rug with. 'Hang on. I'll get my cricket bat.'

The tiger didn't reply. It hung patiently on the clothesline, staring across the lawn, and down towards the creek that bubbled and tumbled noisily through the bottom of the garden. Tim ran into the shed and fetched his bat. When he returned, Hercules was standing at the back door, stretching and yawning.

'Good morning,' Tim said. 'How'd you sleep?'

Hercules ran his hands through his hair. 'Not very well. Your couch is too …'

Tim didn't find out what was wrong with the couch, however, because Hercules suddenly gave a loud yell. 'Beware! A tiger! A vicious, man-eating tiger. Right behind you.'

'No, it's just –'

Pausing only to flex his muscles, the hero rushed to Tim's side. 'Do not fear, Tim Baker, the mighty Hercules will save you!'

'You don't need to save me,' Tim said, prodding the tiger-skin rug with the cricket bat. 'It's not dangerous, it's just a rug.'

'Don't you believe it. Once a man-eater, always a man-eater. And you, my friend, are snack sized.' Hercules pulled the bat out of Tim's hands. He poked at the stuffed head. The rug swayed back and forth on the clothesline. 'See how it threatens us. It prepares to pounce.'

'But it's dead.'

'That's what it wants you to think.' Hercules growled at the tiger. 'You can't fool me, vile beast.'

Tim took his bat back and put it down a safe distance away. 'It's just a –'

'Hah!'

Tim looked on as Hercules dragged the tiger skin to the ground. The hero and the rug rolled around and around the backyard. One moment Hercules was on top; the next moment the rug was. Soil and bits of grass clung to the tiger skin. It was dirtier than ever.

As they tussled, Hercules glared at the tiger's jaws. 'I've beaten mightier foes than you. Even the Lion of Nemea, the most fearsome beast in the world.'

The tiger didn't answer. It flopped bonelessly as Hercules kept rolling and talking.

'That ugly cat was a man-eater. Its hide was so thick, no weapon could pierce it. I was the only one strong enough to defeat it. Do you want to know how I did it?'

The tiger's head nodded.

'Don't try making friends with me,' Hercules hissed. 'You don't fool me that easily.' With one powerful leap, Hercules flipped them both over so that the skin was pinned beneath his knees.

'I didn't need a weapon,' Hercules continued, scowling into the tiger's face. 'I killed it with my bare hands, then I cut through its skin with its own sharp claws. And guess what? I turned that tough lion into a cloak. I'd give up now if I were you.'

Suddenly, there was a loud ripping sound. A long tear appeared in the tiger-skin rug, from its tail to its front paw.

'That's more like it.' Jumping to his feet, Hercules slapped the dirt off his hands. 'Victory is mine.'

Tim groaned. How was he going to fix the rug without Mum finding out?

Hercules picked up the torn skin and examined it. He gave Tim a commiserative glance. 'I hate to say this, my friend, but you were wrong. This is not a man-eater after all! It's just a skin. See?' Hercules slung the rug on like a cloak. The tiger's jaw rested on Hercules' forehead like a hat.

Tim opened his mouth to explain then changed his mind. There was no point. Hercules might be super-strong, but he wasn't super-smart.

'For you.' Hercules took the skin off and wrapped it gently around Tim.

It was hot and heavy and itchy. Tim felt his knees sag from the weight.

'Wear this cloak to school,' Hercules said. 'It shall protect you from arrows.'

'I don't need to be protected from arrows.'

'Of course you do. Skinny little lad like you. You need all the help you can get.'

From *Here Comes Hercules* by Stella Tarakson, published by Sweet Cherry Publishing; reproduced with permission

For questions **1–6**, choose the answer (**A**, **B**, **C** or **D**) which you think best answers the question.

1   The fact that Tim talks to a tiger-skin rug suggests that he
   A feels some sense of the fact that the rug was once a live animal.
   B is frightened of Hercules so pretends the rug is alive.
   C is unable to distinguish between fantasy and reality.
   D is expecting the rug to reply to him.

2   In Greek mythology, Hercules defeated the monstrous Nemean Lion. It is referenced in this story in order to
   A frighten the reader by comparing the tiger to a monster.
   B show that Hercules is trying to relive his past glories.
   C show that the author knows Greek mythology.
   D make the rug appear beautiful by comparison.

3 Hercules is overly concerned for Tim's safety. This shows that
  A Tim lives in a dangerous neighbourhood.
  B Hercules thinks Tim has a powerful enemy.
  C Hercules does not have any children of his own.
  D Ancient Greek society was more dangerous than our modern world.

4 The phrase 'a commiserative glance' tells us that Hercules
  A felt sorry for the tiger.
  B thought Tim would get in trouble for tearing the rug.
  C thought Tim had been mistaken.
  D was super-strong but not super-smart.

5 Tim can be described as
  A timid and easily frightened.
  B hardworking and kind.
  C impatient and argumentative.
  D overly trusting and gullible.

6 What is Hercules's attitude towards Tim?
  A cold and uncaring
  B irritated and angry
  C loving and respectful
  D loving but overprotective

Read the poem below by Heinrich Heine then answer the questions.

The Lorelei

I don't know what it may signify
That I am so sad;
There's a tale from ancient times
That I can't get out of my mind.

The air is cool and the twilight is falling,
And the Rhine is flowing quietly by;
The top of the mountain is flittering
In the evening sun.

The loveliest maiden is sitting,
Up there wondrous to tell.
Her golden jewellery sparkles,
As she combs her golden hair.

She combs it with a golden comb
And sings a song as she does;
A song with a peculiar,
Powerful melody.

It seizes upon the boatman in his small boat
With unrestrained woe;
He does not look below the rocky shoals;
He only looks up at the heights.

If I'm not mistaken the waters,
Finally swallowed up fisher and boat.
And with her singing
The Lorelei did this.

For questions **7–11**, choose the answer (**A**, **B**, **C** or **D**) which you think best answers the question.

7 Lorelei is the name of the
  A river.
  B boat.
  C boatman.
  D beautiful woman.

8 The poem's narrator is feeling sad because
  A he cannot reach the lovely maiden.
  B it is getting cold and dark.
  C he is recalling a tale from ancient times.
  D his boat is capsizing.

9 The phrase 'unrestrained woe' tells us that
  A the boatman was worried about sinking.
  B the song made the boatman feel intensely sad.
  C the lovely maiden was calling out a warning.
  D the boat was starting to break apart.

10 The boat sank because
  A the boatman was not looking where he was going.
  B the boat was too small and unsafe.
  C the water was very rough.
  D the boatman could not bear the singing any longer.

11 The Lorelei appears to be
  A unaware of the effect she has on the boatman.
  B deliberately luring the boatman to his doom with her enticing singing.
  C singing a mournful song because she knows the boat will sink.
  D a figment of the boatman's imagination.

SAMPLE TEST 2

Read the text below then answer the questions.

Six sentences have been removed from the text. Choose from the sentences (**A**–**G**) the one which fits each gap (**12–17**). There is one extra sentence which you do not need to use.

Protecting special places

Some places in the world are so special, they are considered to be of global significance. **12** _____. Such places need to be protected and preserved for the benefit of future generations so many of them have been added to a list of special sites known as the World Heritage List.

A World Heritage Site is one that has been recognised by UNESCO (the United Nations Educational, Scientific and Cultural Organisation) as being of global importance. Only countries that are part of an international agreement called the Convention Concerning the Protection of the World Cultural and Natural Heritage are able to nominate sites for the list. **13** _____. As indicated by the convention's title, a site must be of either natural or cultural significance in order to be nominated.

Not surprisingly, a natural World Heritage Site must be naturally occurring. It must also meet other criteria; for instance, the site must be of exceptional beauty or geological significance. It may be important because it is a habitat for living things and its existence is necessary for biological diversity. It may be home to a threatened species of outstanding universal value, either from the point of view of scientific study or the need for conservation. **14** _____. It is the largest of its kind, contains rare species and is considered one of the seven natural wonders of the world.

Cultural World Heritage Sites must satisfy different criteria. **15** _____. It may be something that shows the traditions and beliefs of a civilisation that is either living or has since disappeared. Often they show the interactions of humans with their environment or are connected to an archaeological dig or research area. Many protected sites contain buildings or monuments of artistic, historic or scientific value. For example, Australia contains many heritage-listed convict sites, such as Port Arthur in Tasmania, that illustrate our rich convict history.

Some sites have both cultural and natural significance. **16** _____. It is a spectacular rock formation that is sacred to the Anangu people and its unique qualities are recognised worldwide.

Some sites are so threatened that they have been placed on the List of World Heritage in Danger. This list exists to warn the international community about an immediate or threatened risk and to encourage protective action to be taken. **17** _____.

A	A cultural site may represent a masterpiece of human creative genius.
B	Even if placed on the list, each site is still owned by the country it is located in.
C	It is a non-profit intergovernmental organisation.
D	They matter to all of humanity, not only to the people who live there.
E	Examples of threats include wars, pollution and natural disasters.
F	For example, Uluru is naturally occurring but has great cultural significance.
G	Australia's Great Barrier Reef is such an example.

Read the four extracts below on the theme of music lessons.

For questions **18–25**, choose the option (**A**, **B**, **C** or **D**) which you think best answers the question.

Which extract …

identifies multiple subsidiary benefits of learning music?	18	_____
suggests that music can be a type of therapy?	19	_____
suggests that music can bring families together?	20	_____
implies that being good at music is an important social skill?	21	_____
describes a change in attitude towards learning music?	22	_____
mentions some specific jargon connected to learning music?	23	_____
reveals that some people are better at music than others?	24	_____
contains a character that does not own a musical instrument?	25	_____

EXTRACT A

At nine they stopped work, and sang, as usual, before they went to bed. No one but Beth could get much music out of the old piano, but she had a way of softly touching the yellow keys and making a pleasant accompaniment to the simple songs they sang. Meg had a voice like a flute, and she and her mother led the little choir. Amy chirped like a cricket, and Jo wandered through the airs at her own sweet will, always coming out at the wrong place with a croak or a quaver that spoiled t'ittle 'tar, and it had become a household custom, for the mother was a born singer. The first sound in the morning was her voice as she went about the house singing like a lark, and the last sound at night was the same cheery sound, for the girls never grew too old for that familiar lullaby.

From *Little Women* by Louisa May Alcott

EXTRACT B

'I am very glad to hear such a good account of her,' said Lady Catherine; 'and pray tell her from me, that she cannot expect to excel if she does not practise a good deal.'

'I assure you, madam,' he replied, 'that she does not need such advice. She practises very constantly.'

'So much the better. It cannot be done too much; and when I next write to her, I shall charge her not to neglect it on any account. I often tell young ladies that no excellence in music is to be acquired without constant practice. I have told Miss Bennet several times, that she will never play really well unless she practises more; and though Mrs Collins has no instrument, she is very welcome, as I have often told her, to come to Rosings every day, and play on the pianoforte in Mrs Jenkinson's room. She would be in nobody's way, you know, in that part of the house.'

From *Pride and Prejudice* by Jane Austen

SAMPLE TEST 2

EXTRACT C

It's easy to forget your problems when you play a musical instrument. I started learning on our piano when I was only four years old. At first, I hated it. Being made to sit inside practising when everyone else was out kicking a ball or playing computer games was awful. Music felt more like a punishment than a privilege, no matter what my mother said. My fingers were still so small, I had to stretch them hard to reach the keys. Often my hands would ache by the end of the day.

However, now I'm so grateful. I still play the piano every day but not because I have to. I don't have to practise for exams anymore, rather I can play the music that I love. Whenever something worries or upsets me, I lose myself completely in my music. What was once a source of stress now transports me to a place of peace and serenity, and I wouldn't give it up for anything.

EXTRACT D

Children derive many benefits from learning how to play a musical instrument that go way beyond mastering the instrument itself. It improves their self-discipline and teaches them to work steadily towards both short- and long-term goals. Setting aside time to practise every day helps them learn to stick to a task, even when the results take a long time to become apparent. This fosters both patience and commitment. Each time they master a new technical skill or learn a new song, they will be rewarded with a sense of pride and achievement, and performing in front of others can help their confidence grow.

There are also many other benefits to be had. Research shows that music lessons improve the way a child's brain functions, ultimately helping them with all aspects of education and learning. Learning an instrument improves a child's memory, logic and reasoning abilities, and helps them develop longer attention spans. It helps their body and mind work together, improving their fine motor skills and enhancing spatial awareness.

Read the text below then answer the questions.

Tom surveyed his last touch with the eye of an artist, then he gave his brush another gentle sweep and surveyed the result, as before. Ben ranged up alongside of him. Tom's mouth watered for the apple, but he stuck to his work. Ben said:

'Hello, old chap, you got to work, hey?'

Tom wheeled suddenly and said:

'Why, it's you, Ben! I warn't noticing.'

'Say—I'm going in a-swimming, I am. Don't you wish you could? But of course you'd druther *work*—wouldn't you? Course you would!'

Tom contemplated the boy a bit, and said:

'What do you call work?'

'Why, ain't *that* work?'

Tom resumed his whitewashing, and answered carelessly:

'Well, maybe it is, and maybe it ain't. All I know, is, it suits Tom Sawyer.'

'Oh come, now, you don't mean to let on that you *like* it?'

The brush continued to move.

'Like it? Well, I don't see why I oughtn't to like it. Does a boy get a chance to whitewash a fence every day?'

That put the thing in a new light. Ben stopped nibbling his apple. Tom swept his brush daintily back and forth—stepped back to note the effect—added a touch here and there—criticised the effect again—Ben watching every move and getting more and more interested, more and more absorbed. Presently he said:

'Say, Tom, let *me* whitewash a little.'

Tom considered, was about to consent; but he altered his mind:

'No—no—I reckon it wouldn't hardly do, Ben. You see, Aunt Polly's awful particular about this fence—right here on the street, you know—but if it was the back fence I wouldn't mind and *she* wouldn't. Yes, she's awful particular about this fence; it's got to be done very careful; I reckon there ain't one boy in a thousand, maybe two thousand, that can do it the way it's got to be done.'

'No—is that so? Oh come, now—lemme just try. Only just a little—I'd let *you*, if you was me, Tom.'

'Ben, I'd like to, honest injun; but Aunt Polly—well, Jim wanted to do it, but she wouldn't let him; Sid wanted to do it, and she wouldn't let Sid. Now don't you see how I'm fixed? If you was to tackle this fence and anything was to happen to it—'

'Oh, shucks, I'll be just as careful. Now lemme try. Say—I'll give you the core of my apple.'

'Well, here—No, Ben, now don't. I'm afeard—'

'I'll give you *all* of it!'

Tom gave up the brush with reluctance in his face, but alacrity in his heart. And while the late steamer Big Missouri worked and sweated in the sun, the retired artist sat on a barrel in the shade close by, dangled his legs, munched his apple, and planned the slaughter of more innocents.

SAMPLE TEST 3

There was no lack of material; boys happened along every little while; they came to jeer, but remained to whitewash. By the time Ben was fagged out, Tom had traded the next chance to Billy Fisher for a kite, in good repair; and when he played out, Johnny Miller bought in for a dead rat and a string to swing it with—and so on, and so on, hour after hour. And when the middle of the afternoon came, from being a poor poverty-stricken boy in the morning, Tom was literally rolling in wealth. He had besides the things before mentioned, twelve marbles, part of a jews-harp, a piece of blue bottle-glass to look through, a spool cannon, a key that wouldn't unlock anything, a fragment of chalk, a glass stopper of a decanter, a tin soldier.

[…]

He had had a nice, good, idle time all the while—plenty of company—and the fence had three coats of whitewash on it! If he hadn't run out of whitewash he would have bankrupted every boy in the village.

Tom said to himself that it was not such a hollow world, after all. He had discovered a great law of human action, without knowing it—namely, that in order to make a man or a boy covet a thing, it is only necessary to make the thing difficult to attain. If he had been a great and wise philosopher, like the writer of this book, he would now have comprehended that Work consists of whatever a body is obliged to do, and that Play consists of whatever a body is not obliged to do.

From *Tom Sawyer* by Mark Twain

For questions **1–6**, choose the answer (**A**, **B**, **C** or **D**) which you think best answers the question.

1 The real reason Tom insisted on painting the fence himself was that
  A he was trying to tempt Ben into wanting to do it.
  B he was a perfectionist and thought Ben couldn't paint properly.
  C he was following Aunt Polly's instructions.
  D he enjoyed nothing more than painting fences.

2 Which of these statements is true?
  A Tom would rather paint the fence than swim.
  B Tom did not consider painting to be hard work.
  C Tom thought people want things that are hard to get.
  D Tom thought he was a better painter than the other boys.

3 Ben offered to help paint the fence because
  A he felt sorry for Tom.
  B he wanted to impress Aunt Polly.
  C he did not want to eat his apple.
  D Tom convinced him that it was desirable.

4 As used in the extract, the word 'alacrity' means
  A anger.   **B** eagerness.
  C misery.   **D** confusion.

5 Tom Sawyer can be described as
  A hardworking and diligent.
  B generous and kind.
  C obedient and well behaved.
  D lazy and cunning.

6 What does the extract suggest is the difference between work and play?
  A how hard the task is
  B whether you get paid to do it
  C whether you are obliged to do it
  D There is no difference between work and play.

Read the poem below by William Wordsworth then answer the questions.

Lines Written in Early Spring

I heard a thousand blended notes,
While in a grove I sat reclined,
In that sweet mood when pleasant thoughts
Bring sad thoughts to the mind.

To her fair works did Nature link
The human soul that through me ran;
And much it grieved my heart to think
What man has made of man.

Through primrose tufts, in that green bower,
The periwinkle trailed its wreaths;
And 'tis my faith that every flower
Enjoys the air it breathes.

The birds around me hopped and played,
Their thoughts I cannot measure:
But the least motion which they made
It seemed a thrill of pleasure.

The budding twigs spread out their fan,
To catch the breezy air;
And I must think, do all I can,
That there was pleasure there.

If this belief from heaven be sent,
If such be Nature's holy plan,
Have I not reason to lament
What man has made of man?

For questions 7–11, choose the answer (**A**, **B**, **C** or **D**) which you think best answers the question.

7 The 'thousand blended notes' refers to
  A the sounds of nature.
  B the sound of a distant battle.
  C the sound of nearby music.
  D the sound of notepaper being torn.

8 What do we learn about the poem's narrator?
  A He finds nature alienating and frightening.
  B He would rather spend time with people than with nature.
  C He feels sad about the way humans treat each other.
  D He is grieving the loss of a loved one.

9 In the narrator's opinion, plants and animals are
  A menacing and dangerous.
  B happy and grateful to be alive.
  C uncaring about the plight of humans.
  D grieving for humanity.

10 The poem ends on a
  A happy and optimistic note.
  B bitter and angry note.
  C confused and uncertain note.
  D sombre and sad note.

11 The overall mood of the poem is
  A agitated and restless.
  B quiet and reflective.
  C menacing and dangerous.
  D miserable and depressed.

SAMPLE TEST 3

Read the text below then answer the questions.

Six sentences have been removed from the text. Choose from the sentences (**A–G**) the one which fits each gap (**12–17**). There is one extra sentence which you do not need to use.

Renewable energy

Australia's energy market is undergoing significant change. **12** _____ . Traditionally, most of our energy has come from non-renewable resources but as a nation we are decreasing our reliance on such resources and shifting towards renewable energy.

Non-renewable resources are those that cannot be made quickly or easily. **13** _____ . Over millions of years, heat and pressure transformed the remains of ancient plants and animals into substances that we now use as fuel. Examples include oil, coal and natural gas. For much of our nation's history, most of our energy came from burning black and brown coal in power stations and transforming it into electricity. Most cars are still petrol driven and vast quantities of natural gas are used in houses for heating and cooking.

Fossil fuels are limited, however, and we are using them faster than they can be created. **14** _____ . It will take thousands, if not millions, of years for more to be created. This scarcity, as well as the fact that fossil fuels create greenhouse gases that accelerate climate change, has caused many to search for and develop renewable, cleaner sources of energy.

Renewable resources are those that can be used without worrying about them running out. **15** _____ . For example, the sun keeps shining and the wind keeps blowing, time and time again. Often they are cleaner than fossil fuels, meaning they cause less pollution and have little or no greenhouse gas emissions.

Solar energy is used in many ways. It can be used to directly heat water in people's houses and to power solar devices such as lights. It can also be used to create electricity through photovoltaic cells. **16** _____ . Many houses in Australia have solar panels made up of these cells installed on their rooftops. This helps householders reduce their reliance on electricity from the power grid, which is generated by more traditional means. Some homes even generate more power than they need, allowing them to sell their excess electricity back to the grid.

Wind energy is another renewable resource. Turbines, some as tall as skyscrapers, use the power of the wind to generate electricity. **17** _____ . Turbines can be placed anywhere where there is a lot of wind, such as on hilltops and in open fields. Placing the windfarms offshore in open water is an increasingly popular option throughout the world.

Source: www.energy.gov.au/government-priorities/energy-supply

---

A   This means they will eventually run out.

B   This reflects increasing concern about the state of the environment and the need for sustainability.

C   As the wind blows, the blades turn, feeding an electric generator.

D   Black coal produces more energy than brown coal.

E   These are mostly fossil fuels, which were formed deep inside the Earth's crust.

F   They replace themselves naturally over time.

G   Made from silicon and other materials, these transform sunlight into electricity.

SAMPLE TEST 3

Read the four extracts below on the theme of headlice.

For questions **18–25**, choose the answer (**A**, **B**, **C** or **D**) which you think best answers the question.

Which extract …

contains someone's childhood recollections?	18	_____
explains the difference between nits and lice?	19	_____
contains a failed attempt to remove headlice?	20	_____
reveals the consequences of not treating headlice?	21	_____
suggests you can have headlice without feeling itchy?	22	_____
shows that headlice have been around for a very long time?	23	_____
uses humour to communicate its message?	24	_____
describes lice as being just one of life's challenges?	25	_____

EXTRACT A

(At school, Mike discovers that he has headlice. He is worried that his head will have to be shaved and he is determined not to let that happen.)

As soon as they got home, Mike sprinted into the backyard. He knew what to do. Checking no-one was looking, he ran to the clothesline and pulled himself up. He hung upside down and fluffed out his hair. Humming a little tune, Mike waited for gravity to suck the lice off his head.

[…]

Gravity hadn't worked, for some reason. His head was still itchy. Maybe the lice were wearing anti-gravity boots. Or maybe they were bungee jumping back onto his head, using his hair as ropes. Shoulders slumped, Mike trudged inside followed by Sandy, their golden retriever.

'You're lucky you're not human,' Mike said to him. 'Kids have too many problems.'

Sandy licked Mike's hand. His big liquid eyes said he understood. He would help, if only he knew how.

'I know you would. Thanks for offering.' Mike patted the long thick hair in the dog's chest. The very long, very thick hair. Mike froze. He had an idea. Maybe Sandy could help after all.

From *Mike the Spike* by Stella Tarakson, published by New Frontier Publishing; reproduced with permission

---

EXTRACT B

Saturday 23 January 1669

But I do trust in God I am pretty well yet, and resolve, in a very little time, to look into my accounts, and see how they stand. So to my wife's chamber, and there supped, and got her cut my hair and look my shirt, for I have itched mightily these 6 or 7 days, and when all comes to all she finds that I am lousy, having found in my head and body about twenty lice, little and great, which I wonder at, being more than I have had I believe these 20 years. I did think I might have got them from the little boy, but they did presently look him, and found none. So how they come I know not, but presently did shift myself, and so shall be rid of them, and cut my hair close to my head, and so with much content to bed.

From *The Diary of Samuel Pepys*, 1669

EXTRACT C

I'll never forget when I had headlice. There was an outbreak at my school and we were given notes asking our parents to check our heads. I didn't think I'd have any; I always wore my hair pulled back in a high ponytail. I didn't share brushes and I never let anyone borrow my hat. So I was totally shocked when mum announced in a grave voice that she'd found some lice. I hadn't felt itchy before but once she said it, my head started to itch like crazy!

The treatment wasn't much fun. Mum had to smear a smelly solution through my hair but the worst part was combing the nits and lice out. Then, as now, I had long, thick, curly hair and the fine-toothed comb kept snagging. It felt like half my hair was being ripped off my head! I never wanted to go through that ever again and I've been fine. Up until now. My daughter started primary school last week and I've noticed she's started to scratch …

EXTRACT D

Headlice are tiny wingless insects that live on the human scalp. Although they don't carry disease, they are unpleasant and uncomfortable. Headlice cannot fly or jump but they spread easily by crawling. Direct head-to-head contact is necessary, such as when children play closely together. A female louse lays several eggs, which are known as nits, every single day. Left untreated, their numbers can rapidly multiply.

If a child has been exposed to headlice, their scalp should be examined thoroughly. Nits can be found close to the scalp. They are pale, pinhead-sized and oval shaped. Unlike dandruff, nits attach firmly to the hair shaft and cannot be easily brushed off. The lice themselves can be either whitish brown or reddish brown.

If spotted, the child's scalp will need to be treated. There are many products on the market, and a fine-toothed comb should be used to remove the lice and eggs. Pharmacists can give advice as to the most appropriate treatment available.

1 If each of these numbers is rounded to the nearest hundred, which number changes the most?

86	111	448	582	713
A	**B**	**C**	**D**	**E**

2 A piece of licorice is 36 cm long. I cut the licorice into two pieces and one piece is twice as long as the other. How long is the shorter part?

A 6 cm

B 12 cm

C 14 cm

D 16 cm

E 9 cm

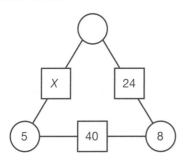

3 The number in each of the squares is the result of multiplying the numbers in the nearest circles.

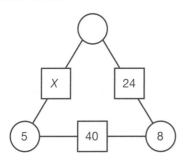

For example, in the bottom row, 5 × 8 = 40. What is the number represented by the letter *X*?

9	20	15	25	35
A	**B**	**C**	**D**	**E**

4 On this number line what number is the arrow pointing to?

124	128	132	136	138
A	**B**	**C**	**D**	**E**

5 The total of Chloe's and Charlotte's ages is 18. If Chloe was 12 when Charlotte was born, how old will Charlotte be in 4 years?

7	6	5	8	10
A	**B**	**C**	**D**	**E**

6 A country's coins come in 1 cent, 5 cents, 10 cents and 25 cents. I have to pay the salesperson $1.07. What is the least number of coins that I can give the salesperson?

7	8	4	6	5
A	**B**	**C**	**D**	**E**

7 Letters are written on a square grid. The square is folded along the dotted line to form a rectangle. The rectangle is then folded along the dotted line to form a square.

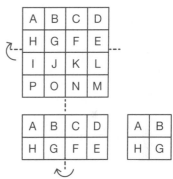

Which of these letters is behind the letter H?

J	L	F	M	K
A	**B**	**C**	**D**	**E**

8 For their class photo, students are arranged according to their height. Levi is the tallest and Elena is the shortest. There are 8 students between Elena and Peyton and 5 students between Grace and Levi. If there are 24 students in the class, how many students are standing between Peyton and Grace?

3	6	5	4	7
A	**B**	**C**	**D**	**E**

9 The frame of a cube is made using wire. Each edge is 5 cm. What is the total length of wire used?

A 48 cm

B 30 cm

C 36 cm

D 72 cm

E 60 cm

10 Jerome is shading squares on the grid.

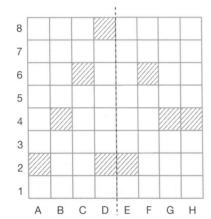

He wants the dotted line to be a line of symmetry where each square on the left reflects to a square on the right. He needs to shade three more squares. Which squares should Jerome shade?

A A4, E8, H3

B A4, E8, H2

C B4, E7, H3

D A4, F8, G2

E B4, E8, H2

11 Which of these pairs of numbers has a total of six factors?

A 1 and 3

B 2 and 4

C 3 and 6

D 2 and 3

E 1 and 8

12 Isabella baked a cake. She cut it into four equal pieces and gave one of the pieces to her friend and two pieces to her neighbour. She then cut the remaining piece into two equal pieces. If Isabella gave one of these pieces to her mother, what fraction of the original cake did her mother eat?

A one-fifth

B one-sixth

C one-eighth

D three-eighths

E one-quarter

13 Look at this multiplication. Each letter stands for a number. Which number could stand for the letter M?

$$\begin{array}{r} MU \\ \times\quad 4 \\ \hline CU8 \end{array}$$

1	5	2	3	4
A	**B**	**C**	**D**	**E**

14 A train left Casino at 7:30 pm and arrived at Central station at 6:45 am the next morning. How long was the train trip?

A 11 hours 15 minutes

B 10 hours 15 minutes

C 10 hours 45 minutes

D 11 hours 45 minutes

E 9 hours 15 minutes

15 Mitchell is using blocks to make steps. This is what he made:

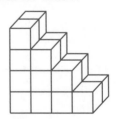

He wants his shape to be 7 blocks high. How many more blocks will he need?

20	24	32	36	18
A	**B**	**C**	**D**	**E**

SAMPLE TEST 1

16 Here is a pattern of numbers:

3814, 4635, 5456, 6277 …

What is the next number in the pattern?

A 7098
B 7198
C 7188
D 7088
E 7076

17 The shape below is made from small identical rectangles. Six of the rectangles are shaded.

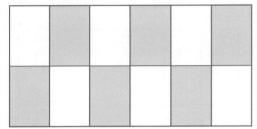

How many more rectangles need to be shaded so that three-quarters of the shape is shaded?

2	3	4	6	9
A	**B**	**C**	**D**	**E**

18 Christopher's parents gave him $10 every time he had no mistakes in his weekly spelling test but if he made a mistake, Christopher would have to pay them $5. At the end of the 10-week term, Christopher was left with $10. How many times did he get full marks in his test?

3	4	6	7	5
A	**B**	**C**	**D**	**E**

19 Clare thinks of a number, adds 8 and then subtracts 4. She then adds another 10. If she ends up with 16, what number did she start with?

5	3	7	6	2
A	**B**	**C**	**D**	**E**

20 The length of a rectangle is twice its width. If the perimeter is 30 cm, what is the area of the rectangle?

A 60 cm²
B 100 cm²
C 75 cm²
D 50 cm²
E 200 cm²

21 Michaela measured the height of her dolls. What is the height difference between her dolls Krystal and Erin?

A 22 cm
B 32 cm
C 26 cm
D 6 cm
E 12 cm

22 Elijah has two bags of coloured balls.

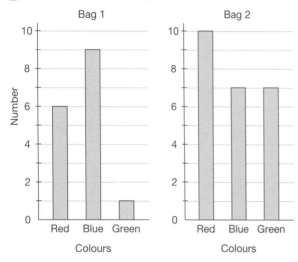

What is the total number of balls in the bags?

28	34	38	40	42
A	**B**	**C**	**D**	**E**

23 Our car's petrol tank holds 60 litres of petrol. We use about 10 litres of petrol for every 100 km we drive. If we start out with a full tank and drive 2000 km, how many times will we have to fill up the tank?

2	3	4	5	6
A	**B**	**C**	**D**	**E**

24 The following scale is balanced.

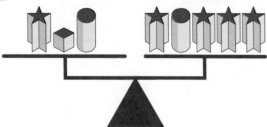

The mass of the is 6 kg.

The mass of the is

A 18 kg   **B** 2 kg   **C** 3 kg

D 4 kg   **E** 6 kg

25 A convenience store sells rice in two different-sized bags. A small bag contains 500 grams and costs $2.50. A larger bag contains 1.5 kg and costs $6. Britt wants to buy exactly 4 kg of rice. What is the smallest amount of money she will need to pay?

A $18

B $16

C $17

D $15.50

E $18.50

26 Here is a 6-by-4 grid.

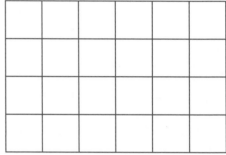

Three friends shaded parts of the grid.

- Myles shaded $\frac{1}{4}$ of the grid squares.

- Pablo shaded $\frac{2}{3}$ of the remaining unshaded squares.

- Finally, Olivia shaded $\frac{1}{2}$ of the remaining unshaded squares.

How many squares on the grid remain unshaded?

0	1	2	3	6
A	**B**	**C**	**D**	**E**

27 Idris's birthday is 3 weeks after Claire's birthday. If Idris was born on 5 July, what date is Claire's birthday?

A 11 June

B 10 June

C 13 June

D 12 June

E 14 June

28 How many of these 10 letters have at least one line of symmetry?

A E H M N S T V W Z

6	7	8	9	10
A	**B**	**C**	**D**	**E**

29 The two rectangles below are joined to make one large rectangle.

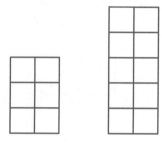

What is the perimeter of the new rectangle?

A 20 units

B 22 units

C 24 units

D 28 units

E 30 units

30 The faces of a cube are numbered 1 to 6. The cube is rolled and the number that is face up is recorded. Here are some statements about the number.

1. It is less likely the number is less than 3 than more than 4.

2. It is more likely the number is a multiple of 3 than a multiple of 2.

3. It is equally likely the number is a factor of 4 or a factor of 6.

Which of George's claims is/are correct?

A statements 1 and 2 only

B statements 1 and 3 only

C statements 2 and 3 only

D statements 1, 2 and 3

E none of the statements

31 Ming rides his bike to work. He rides 4 km north, then 2 km west, 3 km north again and then 7 km east. To get back home what is the shortest way he must ride?

A 7 km south and then 5 km west

B 7 km east and then 5 km north

C 9 km south and then 7 km west

D 9 km east and then 7 km north

E 9 km west and then 7 km south

32 The ten digits 0 to 9 are written in digital form, using only vertical and horizontal lines.

How many right angles are used in writing all the digits that are factors of 6?

11	4	14	16	15
A	**B**	**C**	**D**	**E**

33 Look at the shapes below. They are numbered I, II, III, IV, V and VI.

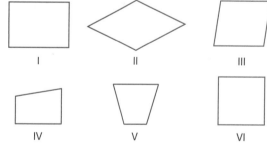

Three of these shapes are joined together to make this pattern. Which shapes were used in the pattern? (Hint: The shapes can be rotated.)

A IV, V, VI

B III, IV, V

C II, IV, VI

D I, V, VI

E I, IV, V

34 Matthew built the following shape by gluing together 38 blocks:

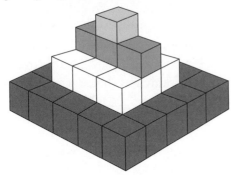

He then glued his shape onto a board and painted the shape blue. How many cubes will not have any blue paint on them?

9	10	11	12	13
A	**B**	**C**	**D**	**E**

35 The number of books read by five students are recorded in the graph below.

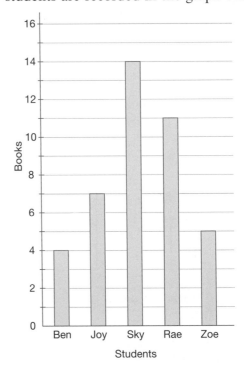

Jake reads the graph and makes three claims.
1. Sky read twice as many books as Joy.
2. Ben and Joy together read the same number of books as Rae.
3. The five students read more than 40 books altogether.

Using the graph, which of Jake's claims is/are correct?

A claim 1 only

B claim 2 only

C claim 3 only

D claims 1 and 3 only

E claims 1, 2 and 3

40 MIN

1 In this magic square, numbers in each row, column and diagonal add to the same total.

10	5	
11		
6		*

What is the value of the *?

12	4	6	13	8
A	B	C	D	E

2 Which number is halfway between 23 and 51?

34	35	36	37	38
A	B	C	D	E

3 James thinks of a number. He adds 4 and doubles the result. When he subtracts 10, his answer is 14. What was James's original number?

10	8	16	6	12
A	B	C	D	E

4 Letters of the alphabet are written using straight or curved lines. Here are six letters:

E T F H L

Three of the letters are chosen at random. What is the smallest possible total number of right angles in the chosen letters?

2	3	4	5	6
A	B	C	D	E

5 One-fifth of a number is 10. Which of these number sentences can be used to find half the number?

A $10 \times 5 \times 2$
B $10 \div 5 \times 2$
C $10 \times 5 \div 2$
D $10 \div 5 \div 2$
E $2 \times 5 \div 10$

6 The following shape is made of 7 identical cubes. It is picked up and dipped in paint. How many cube faces are **not** painted?

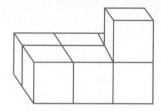

26	35	36	16	12
A	B	C	D	E

7 Claire is using beads to make a necklace. For every 3 red beads, she uses 2 pink beads and a white bead. If she uses a total of 16 pink beads, how many red beads will she use?

17	20	30	32	24
A	B	C	D	E

8 Hassan looked at a triangle with two equal sides, a parallelogram and a square. He counted the number of lines of symmetry on the three shapes. What was Hassan's total?

3	5	7	9	11
A	B	C	D	E

9 April leaves her campsite and walks 2 km east. She then turns and walks 3 km south. She stops for lunch. April then walks 1 km west and 2 km north. In what direction is her campsite?

A south-east
B south-west
C north-east
D north-west
E north

10 The graph shows the height of six schoolfriends.

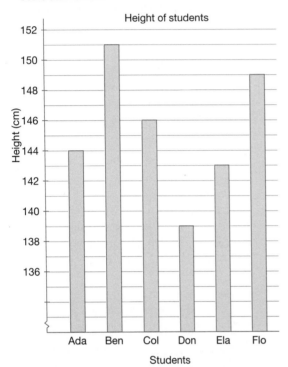

Gemma reads the graph and makes these three claims.

1. Col is 8 cm taller than the shortest student.
2. Ela is the third tallest student.
3. Four students are at least 144 cm tall.

Using the graph, which of Gemma's claims is/are correct?

A claim 1 only
B claim 2 only
C claim 3 only
D claims 1 and 3 only
E claims 1, 2 and 3

11 Here is a number line.

What is the value of $A + C - B$?

30	10	8	20	4
A	**B**	**C**	**D**	**E**

12 A plumber arrived at Lisa's apartment at 11:54 am and left at 1:18 pm. How long was the plumber at the apartment?

A 84 minutes   **B** 86 minutes
C 104 minutes   **D** 106 minutes
E 94 minutes

13 You can park your car in Agora Shopping Centre for the first two hours for free. Then you pay $7 for the next hour and $3 for each hour or part hour after that. Allegra drove into the car park at 10:00 am and left at 1:20 pm.
She put a $50 note into the parking machine. How much change should the machine give her?

$40	$43	$47	$37	$34
A	**B**	**C**	**D**	**E**

14 Abbie has fewer than 60 beads in a jar. When she places them in groups of 3 or 5, she has none left over. But when she places them in groups of 7, she has 2 left over. What is the exact number of beads in the jar?

15	16	23	28	30
A	**B**	**C**	**D**	**E**

15 In this diagram $4 \times 8 = 32$.

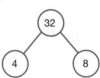

Here is a new diagram that works in the same way:

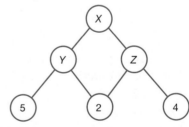

What is the value of X?

6	42	36	80	72
A	**B**	**C**	**D**	**E**

16 There were 16 chocolates in a box. Jannah ate one-quarter of the chocolates on Saturday. She ate half of the remaining chocolates on Sunday. How many chocolates were left in the box?

10	6	8	4	2
A	B	C	D	E

17 The shape consists of 10 identical squares.

Ben shades four of the squares. Jen shades two-thirds of the remaining squares. How many squares remain unshaded?

2	3	4	5	6
A	B	C	D	E

18 This morning, Greg completed 12 push-ups. He plans to increase the number by three every morning. How many push-ups does Greg plan to complete a week from today?

27	28	30	31	33
A	B	C	D	E

19 The school principal needs to randomly choose students to complete a survey. She uses an alphabetical list of 24 student names. She chose every fifth name on the list. How many students were chosen?

2	6	5	4	10
A	B	C	D	E

20 A block of land is 32 m by 16 m. How many rolls of grass 4 m by 2 m will exactly cover the block of land without overlapping?

16 m

32 m

96	128	64	62	60
A	B	C	D	E

21 In this number sentence, ▲ represents a missing number.
63 + ▲ = 48 + 35
What is the value of ▲ ?

20	30	26	28	10
A	B	C	D	E

22 A bag contains 12 balls. Half of the balls are red, three are blue and the remainder are green. Owen chooses a ball at random from the bag.
He makes these three claims.
1. To choose a blue ball or a green ball is equally likely.
2. It is twice as likely that a red ball rather than a blue ball is chosen.
3. Half the red balls are removed from the bag. To choose a red, blue or green ball is equally likely.
Which of Owen's claims is/are correct?

A claim 1 only
B claim 2 only
C claim 3 only
D claims 2 and 3 only
E claims 1, 2 and 3

23 Josh is given a $200 gift card for his birthday. He spends $70 on a video game and $40 on a controller. One-third of the remaining amount is spent at the cinema. What amount of money remains on the gift card?

$25	$20	$30	$40	$60
A	B	C	D	E

24 Cleo has two containers which can hold 400 mL each. Container *A* has 280 mL of water and Container *B* has 180 mL of water. Imogen pours half of the water from Container *A* into Container *B*. How much more water does she need to completely fill Container *B*?

220 mL	70 mL	240 mL	110 mL	80 mL
A	B	C	D	E

25 An unopened jar of peanut butter has a mass of 410 g. When it is half full, the mass is 235 g. What is the mass of the empty jar?

50 g	90 g	70 g	60 g	80 g
A	B	C	D	E

26 Grace has a pan balance and five blocks. The blocks have different masses: 12 kg, 7 kg, 5 kg, 8 kg and 2 kg. Grace used some of the blocks to measure the mass of a cylinder.

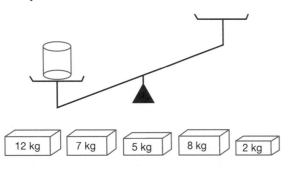

Which of these **cannot** be the mass of the cylinder?

20 kg	21 kg	19 kg	34 kg	23 kg
A	B	C	D	E

27 Trae paints four walls, each with dimensions 5 m by 3 m. Every litre of the paint he is using covers 6 m². How much paint will Trae use?

16 L	8 L	10 L	12 L	6 L
A	B	C	D	E

28 How many of these shapes have at least four lines of symmetry?

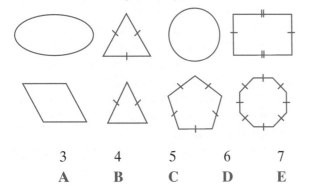

3	4	5	6	7
A	B	C	D	E

29 This year Tameka's birthday is on Tuesday 25 October. Her friend Caitlin has her birthday on 17 November. What day of the week is Caitlin's birthday this year?

A Tuesday   **B** Wednesday
C Thursday   **D** Friday
E Saturday

30 A 28-cm length of wire is cut into two pieces. Both pieces are bent into squares. The larger square has a perimeter of 16 cm. What is the area of the smaller square?

8 cm²	9 cm²	16 cm²	36 cm²	144 cm²
A	B	C	D	E

31 Jess starts with a piece of paper in the shape of a kite, as shown:

She makes **one fold** in the paper, without moving it in any other way.
Which of the following shapes could **not** be the result?

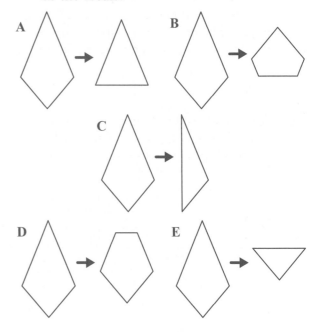

32 A rectangle and a square are both drawn on the grid below. The rectangle has an area of 48 cm². What is the perimeter of the square?

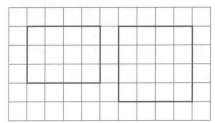

A 16 cm

B 24 cm

C 28 cm

D 32 cm

E 36 cm

33 Jeremiah has a rectangular piece of paper which has a length twice as long as the width. He cuts the paper into two equal shapes. Jeremiah makes three statements.

1. The shapes are both triangles.
2. The shapes are both rectangles.
3. The shapes are both squares.

Which of the statements can be true?

A statement 1 only

B statements 1 and 2 only

C statements 1 and 3 only

D statements 2 and 3 only

E statements 1, 2 and 3

34 How many rectangular prisms are found in this shape?

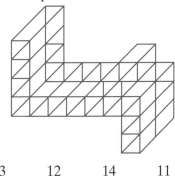

13	12	14	11	10
A	B	C	D	E

35 Students in classes 4P and 5K voted in student elections. The votes for Aria, Levi, Jack and Isla are recorded in the graphs below.

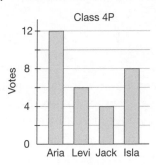

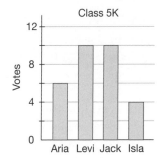

Here are three statements about the graphs.

1. Levi received the same number of votes from the two classes.
2. The same number of students voted in Class 4P as in Class 5K.
3. Isla received the smallest total number of votes from the students in the classes.

Using the information on the graphs, which of the statements is/are correct?

A statement 1 only

B statement 2 only

C statements 1 and 2 only

D statements 2 and 3 only

E statements 1, 2 and 3

40 MIN

1 Jemima buys a carton of eggs costing $5.35. She uses a $10 note to pay for the eggs. What is the smallest number of coins she can be given as change?

2	3	4	5	6
A	B	C	D	E

2 △ , ○ , ▭ and ⬠ represent four **different** whole numbers. All the numbers multiply together to give 24. Which of these could be two of the numbers?

A 2 and 6   **B** 1 and 6   **C** 3 and 8
D 2 and 4   **E** 1 and 8

3 What is the difference in the values of the 4 and the 8 in the number 4853?

40	400	3200	3600	4000
A	B	C	D	E

4 Two numbers add to 100. One of the numbers is 48 more than the other. What is the larger number?

24	26	72	74	76
A	B	C	D	E

5 The diagram shows a grid with a dotted, diagonal line.

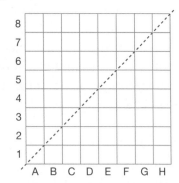

Eve shades these five squares: B2, D3, E8, G7 and H5.
How many more squares does she need to shade for the dotted line to be a line of symmetry?

1	2	3	4	5
A	B	C	D	E

6 A bakery bakes 80 dozen hot cross buns and has them available for sale from 8 am. By 10 am, 20 dozen buns have been sold. Up to 3 pm, another 100 buns each hour are sold. How many hot cross buns remain?

200	420	360	380	220
A	B	C	D	E

7 Here are five digits: 4   7   2   8   5
Nupur uses the digits to make three-digit numbers. How many of her numbers are odd numbers larger than 600?

6	7	8	9	10
A	B	C	D	E

8 Here is a number line.

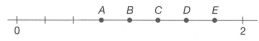

Which letter represents $1\frac{1}{2}$?

A	B	C	D	E
A	B	C	D	E

9 In this puzzle, numbers in opposite squares multiply together to give the number in the middle square.

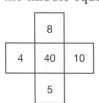

Here is another puzzle that follows the same rule:

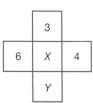

What is the difference between the numbers represented by *X* and *Y*?

24	28	12	32	16
A	B	C	D	E

SAMPLE TEST 3

10 Here are two identical triangles:

Which of the following figures **cannot** be formed by joining the triangles together?

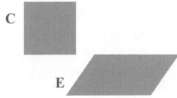

11 This shape is made from six small, identical cubes.

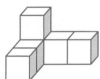

The shape is picked up and viewed from all directions.
How many cube faces **cannot** be seen?

4	6	8	10	12
A	B	C	D	E

12 How many whole numbers between 20 and 50 are multiples of 3?

8	10	11	12	13
A	B	C	D	E

13 What number would replace the * in the table?

2	7	4	6	10
7	17	11	*	23

13	14	16	15	17
A	B	C	D	E

14 A rectangle is formed using four identical squares. The perimeter of the rectangle is 20 cm.

What is the area of each of the squares?
A 8 cm^2
B 2 cm^2
C 5 cm^2
D 25 cm^2
E 4 cm^2

15 The sum of two numbers is 36. If the smaller number is one-third of the larger number, what is the difference between the two numbers?

8	16	18	20	24
A	B	C	D	E

16 In this diagram $12 + 6 = 18$.

Here is a new diagram that works in the same way:

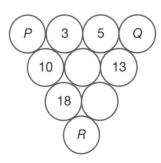

What is the sum of P, Q and R?

52	56	48	58	54
A	B	C	D	E

17 Which of these sequences has 40 as one of its numbers?
A 2, 4, 8, 16 …
B 21, 24, 27, 30 …
C 5, 15, 25, 35 …
D 22, 26, 30, 34 …
E 100, 90, 80, 70 …

18 Byron has made a ruler using a length of cardboard. There are markings on his ruler showing 0 cm, 3 cm, 5 cm, 8 cm and 9 cm.

Byron uses his ruler to measure some lengths. Which of these lengths **cannot** be accurately measured without moving his ruler?
A 1 cm
B 2 cm
C 3 cm
D 4 cm
E 7 cm

19 Here are three shapes *X*, *Y* and *Z*.

Shape *X*   Shape *Y*   Shape *Z*

Which of the shapes has/have $\frac{3}{4}$ shaded?
A shape *X* only
B shape *Y* only
C shape *Z* only
D shapes *Y* and *Z* only
E shapes *X*, *Y* and *Z*

20 Two containers are pictured. Juice has been poured into both containers.

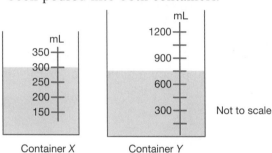

Container *X*   Container *Y*

One-third of the juice from Container *X* is then poured into Container *Y*. How much juice is now in Container *Y*?
A 900 mL
B 850 mL
C 800 mL
D 950 mL
E 1000 mL

21 Kyah is using cans to make a series of towers.

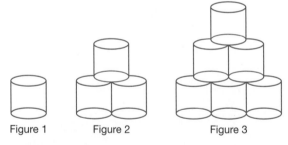

Figure 1   Figure 2   Figure 3

The first figure has 1 can, the second figure has 3 cans, and so on. She continues the series. How many cans will she use in Figure 7?

27	28	25	21	30
A	**B**	**C**	**D**	**E**

22 A laptop's software update is scheduled to take 3 minutes 5 seconds. After 90 seconds, what time remains for the update to complete?
A 215 seconds
B 85 seconds
C 90 seconds
D 95 seconds
E 105 seconds

23 The shape consists of an ellipse in the middle of a square, which is in the middle of a circle. How many lines of symmetry has this shape?

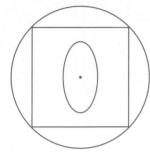

0	1	2	3	4
A	B	C	D	E

24 This year Alex's birthday is on a Sunday. Matthew is 11 days older than Alex. Milan is 23 days older than Matthew. What day of the week is Milan's birthday this year?

A Sunday

B Thursday

C Saturday

D Monday

E Friday

25 The grid shows a bike ride taken by Greta. She started at *A* then rode north to *B*, then to *C*, *D*, *E* and *F*. Greta then rode west to *G* (not shown), which is 10 km south of *A*.

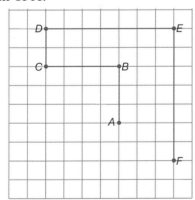

What was the total length of Greta's ride from *A* to *G*?

A 24 km

B 26 km

C 52 km

D 120 km

E 130 km

26 Here is a shape made up of squares. How many right angles are in this shape?

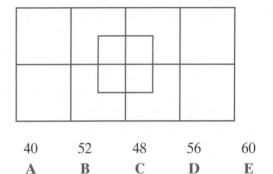

40	52	48	56	60
A	B	C	D	E

27 Sean has a rhombus.

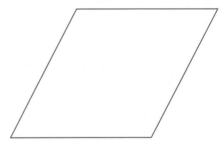

He makes one straight-line cut to divide the rhombus into two shapes. Which of these can he make with the one cut?

1. two triangles

2. two parallelograms

3. a triangle and a hexagon

A 1 only

B 2 only

C 3 only

D 1 and 2 only

E 2 and 3 only

28 A spinner is made using eight equal sectors of a circle.

Frida spins the arrow.
She makes three claims.
1. It is unlikely the arrow will point to the number 6.
2. It is less likely an even number will be spun than an odd number.
3. It is more likely the number 4 will be spun than the number 8.

Which of Frida's claims is/are correct?

A claim 1 only

B claim 2 only

C claim 3 only

D claims 1 and 3 only

E claims 2 and 3 only

29 A sequence of numbers is written using the rule 'Starting with 48, halve the number and add 16'. What is the fifth number in the sequence?

27	28	30	32	33
A	B	C	D	E

30 A survey of students was conducted to find their favourite sports. A pictograph is used to display the results.

Favourite sports

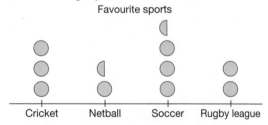

Eight students said their favourite sport was rugby league. How many more students like cricket than netball?

2	3	6	8	10
A	B	C	D	E

31 Here is a large and a small shape. How many of the smaller shapes will fit into the larger shape?

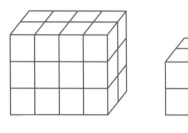

4	5	6	8	7
A	B	C	D	E

32 The mass of two crates is compared. Crate *A* has five times the mass of Crate *B*. If the total mass of the two crates is 30 kg, what is the mass of Crate *B*?

A 12 kg

B 15 kg

C 10 kg

D 6 kg

E 5 kg

33 The diagram below shows a pan balance.

What is the mass of three balls?

A 4 kg

B 8 kg

C 6 kg

D 10 kg

E 12 kg

34 Lily drew a rectangle on the grid below. The perimeter of the rectangle is 32 cm. This meant she could work out the scale used on the grid.

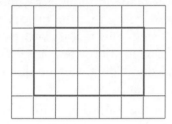

What is the area of the rectangle?

A 160 cm^2

B 40 cm^2

C 60 cm^2

D 20 cm^2

E 80 cm^2

35 Students completed a quiz consisting of 20 questions. The graph shows the number of girls and boys who answered at least 15 questions correctly.

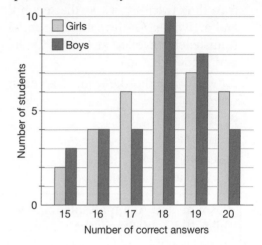

How many more girls than boys scored more than 16 out of 20?

1	2	3	4	5
A	B	C	D	E

1 A train left Herringdale and headed towards Guthrie at 9 am. Another train left Guthrie heading towards Herringdale at the same time. The first train was travelling twice as fast as the second train and arrived at Guthrie at 12 noon. The trains each travelled at a constant speed and made no stops.

At what time did the trains pass each other?

A 10 am

B 10:30 am

C 11 am

D 11:30 am

2 Jasmine and Adam are planning to hike 10 kilometres in the national forest today.

Elle: 'The hike was Jasmine's idea. She hikes all the time. She's fit and she has the endurance. Adam is my best friend and I just know he's going to hate it because it's a tough trail with some steep climbs. I can't believe he agreed.'

Taylor: 'Even though Adam hasn't hiked before, he is very fit from all the mountain biking he does. He has endurance. I think he'll be fine on the hike.'

If the information in the box is true, whose reasoning is correct?

A Elle only

B Taylor only

C Both Elle and Taylor

D Neither Elle nor Taylor

3 The world's oldest bronze factory is in Guanzhuang in China. Archaeologists have been working at the site since 2011, examining evidence of bronze weapons and tools made in the factory and then finding evidence that the factory produced coins as well. This factory proves that China produced bronze coins 2600 years ago and that China was the first country to make bronze coins.

Which of the following sentences, if true, **weakens** the above argument?

A The archaeologists found coins as well as the moulds used to mint them, which is an amazing discovery.

B Until this discovery, most archaeologists believed the world's first coins were made in Turkey or Greece.

C The Chinese site can be dated to 2600 years ago but this doesn't necessarily mean China had the world's first coin factory.

D No-one knows for sure whether coins were originally produced to be able to pay for goods or for governments to be able to collect taxes.

4 At the weekend I am going to the cinema for a Pixar movie marathon. I get to choose one film from each session below.

	Session 1	Session 2	Session 3	Session 4
Cinema 1	Finding Nemo	Monsters Inc.	Toy Story 2	Cars
Cinema 2	Toy Story	Cars	The Incredibles	Toy Story
Cinema 3	Monsters Inc.	Toy Story 2	Monsters Inc.	Finding Nemo
Cinema 4	The Incredibles	Toy Story	Brave	Brave

I know I want to see *Toy Story* and *Toy Story 2* in the correct order and *The Incredibles*. Which movie will I **not** be able to see?

A *Finding Nemo*

B *Monsters Inc.*

C *Cars*

D *Brave*

5 Louella says: 'On the high-altitude Tibetan Plateau, paleontologists are enthusiastically exploring for fossil evidence of one of the largest mammals to roam the earth. Fossils discovered on the plateau are from an animal similar to a rhinoceros. Its skull was one metre long. It was likely taller than a giraffe and would have weighed as much as four elephants. Paleontologists get very excited when they discover new fossils.'

Which of the following statements best expresses the main idea of Louella's text?

A Paleontologists are enthusiastically exploring for fossil remains of one of the largest mammals to roam the earth.

B Paleontologists get very excited when they discover new fossils.

C Fossils have been found on the Tibetan Plateau.

D The largest mammal to roam the earth was similar to a rhinoceros but much larger.

6 Of three students in a class, Priti is taller than Dylan and Mena is shorter than Priti. Which one of the following statements must be true?

A Dylan is the tallest.

B Mena is the shortest.

C Priti is the tallest.

D Dylan is the shortest.

7 Hari is performing his show at a festival which begins on Saturday 4th and ends on Saturday 18th of the same month. He will perform twice a day on Thursdays and Saturdays and have a day off on Mondays. He will perform once every other day of the week. How many times will Hari perform during the festival?

A 15   B 16   C 18   D 19

8 Students were given a choice of theme for the end-of-year class party. They could vote to dress as book characters, famous people or animals. Each student got two votes but they were not allowed to vote for the same option twice. The class will only get to dress up if one of the options is voted for by everyone in the class.

Knowing one of the following would allow us to know the result of the vote. Which one is it?

A Every student voted for either book characters or famous people, or both.

B Only two students voted for famous people.

C Animals was the most popular vote.

D No student voted for both famous people and animals.

9 Jack, Naomi, Andrew and Gemma work for a cleaning company. Naomi might not be able to work tomorrow so the manager has said that if Naomi cannot work then Jack will work in her place. If Naomi does work then Andrew will work in place of Gemma.

If Jack does not work the next day, which of the other three will work?

A Naomi only

B Gemma only

C Jack and Andrew

D Andrew and Naomi

10 The following net is folded into a six-sided dice.

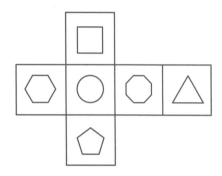

Which of the following is **not** a possible view of the dice?

A 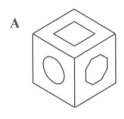   B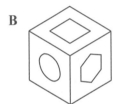

C 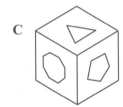   D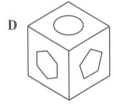

11 The teacher asked students in the class to complete a sociogram questionnaire to explore the friendship groups in the class. Kamala listed her friends as Charli, Tau and Evan. Bailey listed his friends as Elsa, Karol, Anjali, Tau and Evan. Drake listed his friends as Iggy, Elsa, Tau, Harry and Evan.

Which friends did Bailey list that neither Drake nor Kamala listed?

A Elsa and Karol

B Anjali and Tau

C Harry and Charli

D Karol and Anjali

12 Harrison said: 'I think homemade ice cream tastes better than shop-bought ice cream because when you make it yourself, you can use exactly the ingredients you want.'

Which one of these statements, if true, best supports Harrison's claim?

A Homemade ice cream doesn't need the preservatives that help ice cream last longer in the shop.

B When you make ice cream at home, you can use the freshest ingredients and you don't need preservatives.

C Homemade chocolate ice cream with lots of chocolate chips is the best-tasting ice cream.

D Plan when to make your ice cream so you allow time for cooling and freezing.

13 A square piece of paper is folded in half to make a rectangle. This rectangle is folded in half to make a square. These two steps are repeated once. The piece of paper is unfolded and is cut along all the folds. How many small paper squares are there?

A 4   B 8   C 16   D 32

14 A nutritionist has suggested that all school children be provided with a nutritious hot lunch at school. She believes many school children are not eating enough vegetables and other healthy foods while at school and their academic performance is suffering as a result.

Which of these statements, if true, best supports the nutritionist's claim?

A Good nutrition improves students' ability to learn.

B Some families struggle to provide nutritious food for their children.

C Children will enjoy a hot nutritious lunch while at school.

D Some schools overseas already provide hot lunches.

15 Phil, Chantelle, Lana, David, Birender and Miriam are sitting, spaced evenly around a circular table. Phil is sitting next to both Lana and Birender. David is next to Chantelle.

Who **cannot** be sitting directly opposite Chantelle?

A Phil **B** Lana
C Birender **D** Miriam

16 Look at the unfinished square puzzle below:

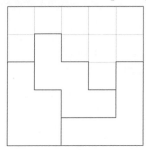

Two of the following shapes are needed to complete the square shown. Shapes may be flipped and rotated.

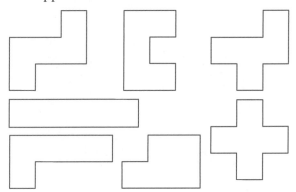

Which of the shapes can definitely **not** be used?

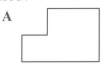 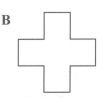

 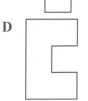

17 In an effort to increase coffee production, millions of hectares of Indonesia's native forests are being replaced with farms. Expanding farmland has resulted in reduced habitats for wildlife, such as Sumatran tigers, rhinos and elephants, but in South Sumatra there is a growing trend for sustainable coffee farms. These can coexist with native forests and protect the environment in other ways.

Which one of these statements, if true, **weakens** the above argument?

A Sumatran tigers are an endangered species.
B Sustainable farming ensures farmers and workers are fairly paid.
C Coffee pulp can fertilise the soil on a sustainable farm so nothing is wasted.
D The demand for coffee increases globally every year.

18 Tallai Creek State School has won this year's sustainability award. Students at the school planted indigenous vegetation along a tributary of Tallai Creek.

Chiho: 'Native plants are generally better than non-native plants in all ecosystems.'
Obama: 'Indigenous vegetation must be good for sustainability.'
Pippa: 'Native plants help control erosion.'
Sage: 'Indigenous plants have evolved to suit particular environments.'

If the information in the box is true, whose reasoning is correct?

A Chiho **B** Obama
C Pippa **D** Sage

19 The award for the Most Improved in Shotput in each age group at a local athletics club goes to the athlete who has improved his personal best (PB) by the greatest distance since the beginning of the year.

At the beginning of the year the personal bests of the five U14 athletes were as follows:

Graham	5.3 m
Patrick	6.2 m
Ashvin	9.2 m
Johan	5.6 m
Kyle	7.1 m

Their personal bests after one year of competition are shown here:

Graham	6.9 m
Patrick	6.9 m
Ashvin	9.4 m
Johan	7.1 m
Kyle	8.0 m

Who won the award for Most Improved in Shotput?

A Graham   **B** Ashvin
C Johan   **D** Kyle

20
> Whenever all students in class 4C complete their work ahead of time and at an exceptional standard, it makes the teacher very happy with the class. Whenever the teacher is feeling very happy with the class, she rewards the students with a games afternoon for the last hour on the Friday of that week.

Jed: '4C had an indoor games afternoon last Friday. Everyone must have finished their work early and to an exceptional standard.'

Grigor: 'If they finish early and to an exceptional standard this week I'm sure they will have a games afternoon this Friday too.'

If the information in the box is true, whose reasoning is correct?
A Jed only
B Grigor only
C Both Jed and Grigor
D Neither Jed nor Grigor

21
> If you want to be allowed to audition for the choir, you have to attend the information session at 8 am on Wednesday.

Chester: 'I can't attend the information session at 8 am on Wednesday because I have gymnastics at that time so I won't be able to join the choir.'

Gabriella: 'I will attend the information session so I will get into the choir.'

Whose reasoning is correct?
A Chester only
B Gabriella only
C Both Chester and Gabriella
D Neither Chester nor Gabriella

22 In a full set of dominoes, every piece is unique. Each domino is made of two squares, with each square showing a 0 (blank), 1, 2, 3, 4, 5 or 6. There is a domino for every possible combination of those numbers.

This domino has a square showing 2 and a square showing 6:

To play, a domino must be placed at either end of a string of dominoes so that the numbers match. That is, a blank square can only connect to a blank square, a 1 can only connect to a 1, and so on. You can see below an example of a string of dominoes mid-game:

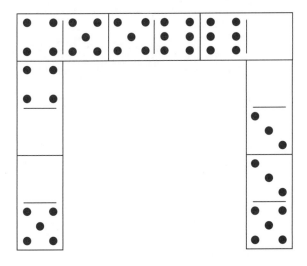

The next player must play a domino at one end of the string; that is, they must play a domino that has a five on it.

How many dominoes with a five on it could the next player choose from?

A 0

B 1

C 2

D 3

23 From his starting point, Angus walked 100 m north, then 200 m west, 200 m south, 300 m east, 100 m south and then 100 m west.

How far will he have to walk, and in which direction, to get back to his starting point? Use the compass below to help you.

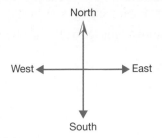

A 200 m north

B 100 m north

C 200 m north-west

D 100 m north-east

24

Shantay: 'It's Hetty's birthday on the 30th.

Amar: 'She's organising putt-putt golf at Golf World for her birthday party.'

Shantay: 'Hetty must like putt-putt golf.'

Which one of the following sentences shows the assumption Shantay has made?

A Hetty must like putt-putt golf.

B Hetty is organising putt-putt golf for her birthday party.

C If someone organises an activity for their birthday, it will be something they enjoy doing.

D Golf World holds children's birthday party celebrations all the time.

25 Peter wants to make as many party sausage rolls as possible from the ingredients he has at home.

He has found a recipe to make 16 sausage rolls using two sheets of puff pastry, 250 g of mince, four carrots and two eggs.

He has nine sheets of pastry, 1 kg of mince, 10 carrots and six eggs at home.

How many sausage rolls can he make?

A 24

B 32

C 40

D 48

26

Farid: 'We're having a huge family gathering on Sunday to meet my cousin's new baby. My great-grandmother and my grandmother and all the aunties and uncles will be coming.'

Chloe: 'Your family must be cooking up mountains of delicious food in preparation. Yummy!'

Which one of the following sentences shows the assumption Chloe has made?

A All Farid's extended family gathers to welcome new babies.

B Family gatherings are fun.

C Farid's family will be cooking up delicious food.

D Farid's family has delicious food at huge family gatherings.

27 Three cards are placed on a table, as shown below. Each card has a white side and a blue side.

A move is made when two cards are flipped over.

You are allowed to make as many moves as you want. Which of the following arrangements of cards will you **never** see?

A

B

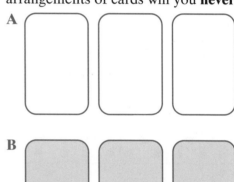

C

D

28 The view of a single-storey building is shown below.

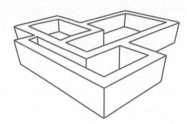

Which of the following diagrams could be the floor plan for this building?

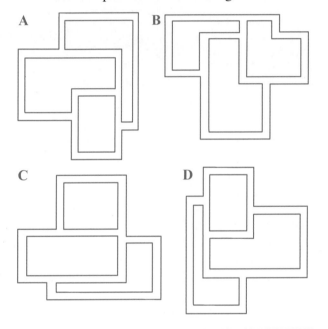

29 Bridgitte is told by her brothers that her birthday present is in one of five coloured boxes in a row. They give her clues to help her find it as they say she only gets one guess.

- The red box is next to the box that contains the present.
- The white box is on the far left and there is only one box between it and the green box.
- There is only one box between the orange box and the box that contains the present.
- The black box is next to the orange box.

Which box should Bridgitte open to find her present?

A white

B green

C orange

D black

30 Roald Dahl is one of the most popular children's authors in the world. He died in 1990 but his books live on, entertaining current and future children all over the world in many languages. His stories mainly involve child heroes who have to deal with grown-ups that are not nice, as in *Matilda, George's Marvellous Medicine* and *The Witches*. Dahl's stories are humorous but also sometimes a bit sad. The made-up words he used in *The BFG* are very clever and I think *George's Marvellous Medicine* is especially funny.

Which of the following best expresses the main idea in the text?

A Roald Dahl is one of the most popular children's authors in the world.

B Roald Dahl's stories mainly involve child heroes who have to deal with grown-ups who are not nice.

C Books written by Roald Dahl include *Matilda, George's Marvellous Medicine, The Witches* and *The BFG*.

D Roald Dahl's stories are humorous but sometimes a bit sad.

1 Two trains departed London for Sunderland at 11 am. One train travelled on the coast line and the other travelled on the inland line. The coast line is 1.5 times as long as the inland line. The trains travelled at the same constant speed and made no stops along the way.

If the train that went on the coast line arrived at 4 pm, what time did the other train arrive?

A 1:30 pm   B 2:20 pm
C 2:30 pm   D 3:20 pm

2 A doctor has warned that young children can suffer a range of injuries if they fall out of highchairs. The doctor recommends a five-point harness system that goes over the infant's shoulders, around their waist and between their legs.

Which one of these statements, if true, best supports the doctor's claims?

A Infants often try to climb from highchairs.

B Infants are much less likely to suffer an injury if they are harnessed correctly.

C Modern highchairs usually offer some level of restraint.

D Safer highchairs are now more readily available than in the past.

3 Maddie says: 'It's easy to grow tomatoes at home.'

Which one of these statements, if true, **weakens** Maddie's argument?

A Tomatoes have high nutritional value.

B Tomatoes can be grown in the home garden without the need for pesticides, which is good news for the environment.

C There are numerous common problems encountered by people growing tomatoes at home so follow the advice of the experts for simple remedies.

D Tomato plants are very productive, yielding many tomatoes each season.

4 At a school camp I wanted to complete the rock climbing, the orienteering, the high ropes and the assault course activities. Below is the timetable for the activities.

Session 1	Session 2	Session 3	Session 4
Abseiling	Orienteering	High ropes	Archery
Low ropes	Rock climbing	Orienteering	High ropes
High ropes	Archery	Assault course	Low ropes
Assault course	Low ropes	Archery	Abseiling

If I got to take part in all my chosen activities, what activity was I doing in Session 3?

A High ropes

B Orienteering

C Assault course

D Archery

5 An ice-cream manufacturer conducted a survey to decide which new flavour to add to its product line. It could only add one new flavour. The five top new flavours were:

Gingerbread swirl

Three berry ripple

Magic mountain mint

Triple trouble luxe

Rolling in the dough

The ice-cream manufacturer found that:

• Triple trouble luxe was more popular than Magic mountain mint.

• Everyone preferred Magic mountain mint to Rolling in the dough.

• Gingerbread swirl was more popular than Three berry ripple.

• Rolling in the dough was preferred over both Gingerbread swirl and Three berry ripple.

Based on the above information, which new flavour will be added to the product line?

A Three berry ripple

B Gingerbread swirl

C Rolling in the dough

D Triple trouble luxe

6 Four friends are sitting in a row at the football. As we look at them, Tim is further left than Connor, Jules is further right than Tim, and Connor is sitting directly to the left of Kylie.

Which one of the following statements **cannot** be true?

A Tim is sitting at one end of the row.

B Kylie is sitting at one end of the row

C Jules is sitting at one end of the row.

D Connor is sitting at one end of the row.

7 The month of March has 31 days in it. April has 30 days. Gobi's birthday is on 4 May. If it's Monday 3 March today, on which day of the week will Gobi's birthday fall?

A Sunday   B Monday

C Wednesday   D Friday

8 The owners' corporation in a block of units can reasonably refuse to allow a pet to live in a unit in the building if they can prove the animal regularly and consistently interferes with another resident's use and enjoyment of their unit or the property's common areas, such as foyers and gardens.

Pandora: 'I'm sure the owners of the dog in unit 8 will probably be notified before long that their dog won't be allowed to live in the building if it continues to bark all day Monday to Friday, while its owners are at work. It annoys everyone.'

Tristan: 'The owners' corporation can't be unreasonable though. The dog would have to be continually interfering with other residents' enjoyment of their units. If the dog barked every now and then, it would be unreasonable to tell its owners it could not live in the building.'

If the information in the box is true, whose reasoning is correct?

A Pandora only

B Tristan only

C Both Pandora and Tristan

D Neither Pandora nor Tristan

9

Hikaru: 'I'll print that document for you later in the week when my new printer arrives.'

Elisabeth: 'Would you like me to take the old one to a recycling facility?'

Which one of the following sentences shows the assumption Elisabeth has made?

A The old printer is broken.

B The new printer will print better-quality documents.

C The old printer could be worth money second hand.

D The new printer will arrive in a few days.

10 The following net is folded into a six-sided dice:

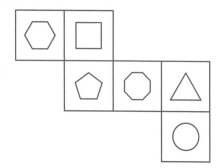

Which of the following is **not** a possible view of the dice?

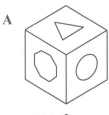
A

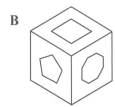
B

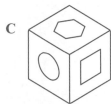
C

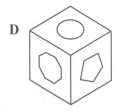
D

11 Sustainable insect farms benefit the environment and edible insects provide humans and animals with a good source of protein. Insect farming reduces the amount of land required for farming livestock animals and therefore helps save forests. Insects do not produce the methane produced by livestock so this helps reduce climate change. Insect farming also saves water.

Which sentence is the main idea in the paragraph?

A Sustainable insect farms benefit the environment.

B Edible insects provide humans and animals with a good source of protein.

C Insects have less fat and more protein than chicken, which makes them healthier to eat.

D Insect farming also saves water.

12 Chantelle plans to sell her bike and buy a new one. In order to sell it for the best price, she has to clean it and make sure it's in good working order. If she doesn't clean it properly, it will not sell for a good price and she won't be able to afford the new bike she wants as she doesn't have enough savings. If she sells her bike but doesn't get enough money for it, she will be without a bike altogether for some time until she saves more money. It will be difficult to get to school without a bike.

Which one of the following statements is **not** possible?

A Chantelle sold the bike and bought a new bike.

B Chantelle sold the bike but did not buy a new bike.

C Chantelle cleaned the bike and checked it was in good working order but it did not sell.

D Chantelle did not clean the bike or check that it was in good working order but it sold for a good price.

13 On a stringed instrument if a string is halved in length, the note that is made by playing it will be higher by one octave. A string that is 3 cm in length is played to make a note. If the length of the string is increased to 24 cm, what change will be heard in the note?

A The note will be 3 octaves lower.

B The note will be 8 octaves lower.

C The note will be 3 octaves higher.

D The note will be 8 octaves higher.

14 Monkeys and apes are primates like humans. There are hundreds of different species of monkey. Almost every kind of monkey has a tail. No ape has a tail. The five species of ape are gibbon, gorilla, chimpanzee, bonobo and orangutan.

Hudson: 'If it's a primate, doesn't have a tail and is definitely not human, gibbon, chimpanzee, bonobo, orangutan or gorilla then it's a monkey.'

Sana: 'If it's a non-human primate that doesn't have a tail, it's definitely an ape.'

If the information in the box is true, whose reasoning is correct?

A Hudson only

B Sana only

C Both Hudson and Sana

D Neither Hudson nor Sana

15 Pierre, Carl, Isaac, Ada, Emmy and Rene are sitting around the rectangular table shown.

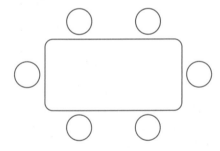

- Rene is sitting directly opposite Carl.
- Pierre is sitting next to Emmy.
- Ada is sitting directly opposite Emmy.
- Isaac is sitting diagonally opposite Rene.

Who is Ada sitting between?

A Pierre and Rene

B Rene and Carl

C Isaac and Carl

D Pierre and Isaac

16 The three shapes below can be arranged to form a three-by-five rectangle as shown:

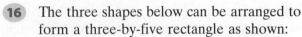

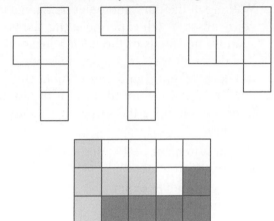

Three of the following shapes can also be arranged to form a three-by-five rectangle. Which shape **cannot** be used?

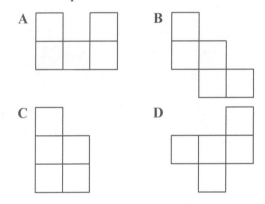

17 The new farmer's market claims that shopping at their market is the healthiest way to buy produce, other than growing your own.

Which one of these statements, if true, **least** supports the claim made by the farmer's market?

A The produce at the market is locally grown and freshly harvested.

B Most of the produce sold at the market was grown using pesticides.

C The produce at the market is ripened before harvesting to optimise vitamins.

D The markets are only held once a month and are cancelled if it rains.

18 People are creatures of daylight. We should go out and experience the dark more often. Walking in the dark and quiet heightens all your senses. You'll experience the sights, sounds and smells of the neighbourhood in a different way. If you are nervous in the dark, take a friend and a torch. But don't talk and try not to turn on the torch. Simply experience the surprising beauty of the dark.

Which statement best expresses the main idea of the argument?

A People should experience the dark more often.

B People are creatures of the light.

C Some people are nervous in the dark.

D Do not talk when you are walking in the dark.

19

Lola: 'If I lose another hat, my mum will get really upset.'

Ramesh: 'You must not lose your hat!'

Which assumption has Ramesh made in order to draw his conclusion?

A Lola will keep losing hats.

B Lola does not like hats.

C Lola's mum will be upset if Lola loses another hat.

D Lola should not do something that would upset her mum.

20 The Most Improved Shooter award in a basketball team goes to the player who improves her point-scoring rank among her team members by the largest number of positions.

At the end of 2020, the average points per game were:

Cayla	24
Tess	23
Kelsey	18
Lauren	15
Jenna	10
Ezi	9
Sara	6
Nneka	4

At the end of 2021, the average points per game for the same team were:

Cayla	19
Tess	28
Kelsey	10
Lauren	15
Jenna	11
Ezi	13
Sara	5
Nneka	9

Who won the Most Improved Shooter award?

A Tess   B Lauren   C Ezi   D Nneka

21 When Santi was learning to scuba dive, her instructor told her: 'To have even a chance of being certified, you must complete both closed-water and open-water dives plus pass the written exam.'

If Santi's instructor is correct, which one of these statements will be true?

A All the scuba divers who have completed open-water dives will be certified.

B Some of the scuba divers who have not completed closed-water dives might be certified.

C None of the scuba divers who have not completed open-water dives will be certified.

D All the scuba divers who pass the written exam will be certified.

22 Dominoes are to be arranged into a square as shown below so that neither of the numbers on a domino are placed next to the same number on another domino.

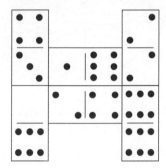

The square is to be completed by choosing from dominoes 1 to 5 below. The same domino cannot be used twice.

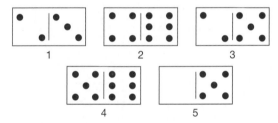

Which two dominoes will **not** complete the square shown?

A 1 and 4
B 2 and 3
C 2 and 4
D 4 and 5

23 In a region, Town C is 10 km due north of Town B, Town A is 10 km due north of Town D, Town B is 10 km due west of Town A, and Town A is 20 km due east of Town E.

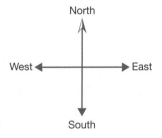

What else is true?

A Town E and Town B are 30 km apart.
B Town C is north-east of Town A.
C Town D is south-west of Town B.
D Town E is south-west of Town C.

24 Dylan's dad likes to run. Whenever he wins a race, it always puts him in a good mood.
And when Dylan's dad is in a good mood, he always sings old songs.

Dylan: 'Dad's singing old songs now—he must have won a race!'

Zara: 'If Dad wins the race on Saturday, he's sure to sing old songs again!'

If the information in the box is true, whose reasoning is correct?

A Dylan only
B Zara only
C Both Dylan and Zara
D Neither Dylan nor Zara

25 Jillian wanted to buy as many tennis balls as she could to practise her game. She went to the shops with $40.

Single ball	3-pack	4-pack	10-pack
$4	$9	$11	$25

What is the maximum number of balls she can buy?

A 15
B 14
C 13
D 10

26 The politician said that the new tunnel would be a huge benefit to the local community.

Which one of these statements, if true, best supports the politician's claim?

A Twenty houses will need to be demolished to build the tunnel.

B Exhaust chimneys for the tunnel will be located next to the local school.

C The tunnel will make travel time to the city much faster.

D No shops will need to be relocated to build the tunnel.

27 Four cards are placed on a table as shown below. Each card has a white side and a blue side.

A single move consists of turning over three cards.

After three moves, which is the only arrangement that is possible?

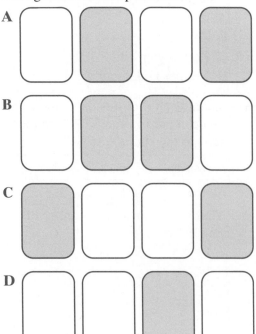

28 The view of a single-storey building is shown below:

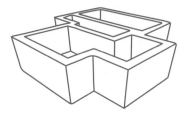

Which of the following diagrams could be the floor plan for this building?

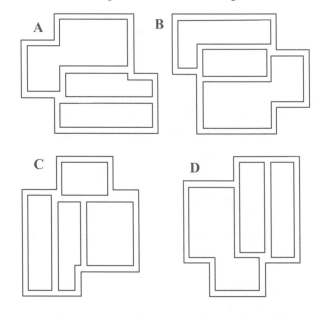

29 Five friends—Alexis, Bella, Carlos, Dave and Emily—live in consecutive houses in a street.

Dave lives two doors from Emily.

Alexis lives three doors from Emily.

Carlos lives in the house farthest to the right.

Alexis and Carlos don't live next door to each other.

In which house does Bella live?

A first house on the left

B second house from the left

C third house from the left

D fourth house from the left

30

Mr Flint: 'I know that 15 of the children in my class have library books due but I only saw eight carrying library bags this morning. So some of the class must have forgotten their library books.'

Which one of the following sentences shows the mistake Mr Flint has made?

A He did not say which children must have forgotten their library books.

B He did not count the children in other classes.

C Some of the other children in the class might want to borrow a library book.

D Some of the children might have brought their books in a different bag.

SAMPLE TEST 3

30 min

1 Two cars competed in a 20-lap race around a circuit. The Ferrari can finish 10 laps in 30 min. The Porsche can finish 15 laps in the same time. If the cars drove at a constant speed and there were no pit stops or accidents, by how many minutes did the Porsche beat the Ferrari?

A 5 min   **B** 10 min
C 20 min   **D** 30 min

2 Human bodies are designed to breathe in through the nose. Breathing in through the nose warms the air before it hits the lungs. The nose also filters out debris and pollutants in the air so they don't reach your lungs. Instead they go down the throat to the stomach but that's better than to the lungs. If you wake in the night with a dry mouth, you might be breathing through your mouth instead of your nose—and missing out on all the benefits of nasal breathing.

Which statement best expresses the main idea of the text?

A If your mouth is dry, you might be breathing through your mouth.

B Human bodies are designed for nasal breathing.

C The nose filters out debris and pollutants.

D Breathing through the nose helps us take deeper breaths.

3 When Loren was learning to sail, her instructor told her: 'To have even a chance of passing the course you must understand all emergency equipment and precautions, including person overboard recovery.'

If Loren's instructor is correct, which one of these statements will be true?

A All the students who understand person overboard recovery will pass the course.

B Some of the students who do not understand person overboard recovery will pass the course.

C Only the students who do not understand person overboard recovery will pass the course.

D None of the students who do not understand person overboard recovery will pass the course.

4 At a holiday creative arts workshop, I can choose a course from each list.

List 1	List 2	List 3	List 4
Ceramics	Sketching	Animation	Textiles
Portraiture	Landscape painting	Ceramics	Lino printing
Sketching	Portraiture	Landscape painting	Working with wood
Lino printing	Working with wood	Textiles	Animation

I know that I want to choose Ceramics, Textiles and Lino Printing.

Which of the following can I **not** choose as my last course?

A Animation
B Portraiture
C Working with wood
D Sketching

5

Ayla: 'I'm going to do my project on dinosaurs.'

Monti: 'You must know a lot about dinosaurs!'

Which one of the following sentences shows the mistake Monti has made?

A Ayla was allowed to choose her own project topic.

B Ayla does not like dinosaurs.

C Students only do projects on topics they know a lot about.

D Choosing a project topic is difficult.

6 Of three TVs, the Screensource is more expensive than the Visionary, and the Visionary is less expensive than the Tellysonic. Which of the following statements must be true?

A The Screensource is the most expensive.

B The Screensource is the second most expensive.

C The Tellysonic is the most expensive.

D The Visionary is the least expensive.

7 Xander is an acrobat in a circus that is showing from Thursday 15th to Saturday 31st of the same month. The circus has a single performance every day except Tuesday, and two performances on Saturdays and Sundays.

If Xander couldn't perform on the 19th due to injury, but performed in every other show, how many times did he perform in the circus?

A 16

B 17

C 18

D 19

8 A tour company suggested that their new weekend package staying in a forest would be good for participants' health.

Which one of these statements, if true, best supports the tour company's claim?

A Participants will be taught how to forage for food and only eat what they find.

B Participants will stay in log cabins.

C Research suggests that time spent in a forest boosts the human immune system.

D Forests are beautiful and there are not many old-growth forests remaining.

9 Tammy saw a single dice from one angle. What she saw is shown below.

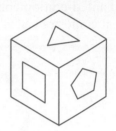

Which **cannot** be the net of the dice?

A
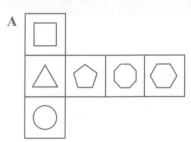

B
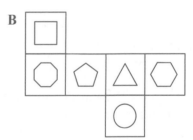

C
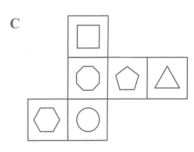

D
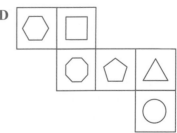

10 Only those customers who have over 100 loyalty points will be allowed to buy the new limited-edition collectable model that comes out next week.

Blake: 'Carlos has 150 loyalty points so he will definitely buy the model next week.'

Mia: 'Evie has 60 loyalty points so she won't be able to buy the new model.'

If the information in the box is true, whose reasoning is correct?

A Blake

B Mia

C Both Blake and Mia

D Neither Blake nor Mia

11 A doctor says: 'Pets are good for people's physical and mental wellbeing.'

Which one of these statements, if true, **least** supports the doctor's claim?

A Pets are great stress relievers.

B Walking a dog is good exercise.

C Some people are allergic to cats or dogs.

D Pets make you laugh and laughter is good for you.

12 Ria was deciding what to have for dinner.

Ria: 'I'd like some pizza. But if I can't have pizza, then I'll have leftovers from last night. And if I do have pizza, then I'll have a salad instead of chips.'

If Ria does not have leftovers, what will she have for dinner?

A salad and chips

B pizza and salad

C pizza only

D salad only

13 A square piece of paper is folded in half along the diagonal to make a triangle. This triangle is folded in half along its line of symmetry to make another triangle. This is done twice more, creating a small triangle.

If the long side of the small triangle is 5 cm long, what is the side length of the original square piece of paper?

A 5 cm B 10 cm C 15 cm D 20 cm

14

Sara: 'Uma won't be able to come to the movies with us. She plays netball every Saturday.'

Joe: 'Uma must love playing netball.'

Which assumption has Joe made in order to draw his conclusion?

A Uma has already seen the movie and does not want to see it again.

B Uma won't go to the movies with Sara and Joe.

C Uma must love playing netball.

D Anyone who plays netball every Saturday loves playing netball.

15 John, Paul, George and Ringo are each sitting on one side of a small square table. There is a window behind one of the chairs.

• George is sitting next to Ringo.

• John has his back to the window.

What else must be true?

A Ringo is facing the window.

B Paul is sitting next to George.

C John is sitting next to Ringo.

D Paul is not facing the window.

16 To cover a four-by-four grid (on the left), four copies of the long rectangle (middle) were used, as shown in the diagram (on the right).

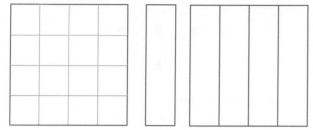

We can also use four copies of three of the following shapes to cover the grid.

For which of the following shapes is this **not** possible?

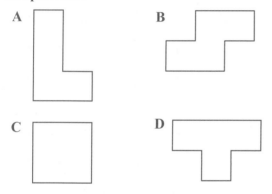

17 Tony says: 'Live-to-air television is better than streaming because it's more exciting. With live to air, you see things as they are happening.'

Which one of these statements, if true, best supports Tony's claim?

A With live television everyone finds out at the same time what happened.

B It's fun to binge a whole series instead of having to wait for the next episode.

C Live-to-air television has advertising.

D You can stream a television show any time you want.

18 Only those musicians who have attended every band practice this term will be allowed to go to the concert at the Town Hall.

Quan: 'I missed band practice last week so I won't be able to go to the Town Hall concert.'

Aziz: 'I've been to every band practice this term so I'll definitely be allowed to go to the Town Hall concert.'

If the information in the box is true, whose reasoning is correct?

A Quan only

B Aziz only

C Both Quan and Aziz

D Neither Quan nor Aziz

19 Jarrod wants to buy a new electric lawnmower at a sale at the hardware store. He can't choose between five models so he decides to buy the model that has the largest saving in dollars. The prices are listed below.

Model	Original price	Sale price
Mowfast	$729	$599
Lawnshort	$595	$445
Blades-begone	$379	$199
First Cut	$1060	$899
Victory	$799	$609

Which lawnmower will Jarrod buy?

A Mowfast   B Blades-begone

C First Cut   D Victory

20 Arlo, Lucy and Suma want to build a treehouse. Arlo wants the treehouse to have a bridge, rope ladder, periscope, slippery dip and bucket pulley. Lucy wants it to have a zipline, bucket pulley and slippery dip. Suma wants a rope ladder, trap door, slippery dip, swing and bucket pulley.

Which treehouse feature does Arlo want that neither Lucy nor Suma want?

A rope ladder and bridge
B periscope and slippery dip
C swing and zipline
D bridge and periscope

21 Bree's mother is in the sports store.

Bree's mother: 'Bree wants a skateboard for her birthday. She said she saw the one she wants in the sports store but I can't seem to find it. She said it has a green design with a shark.'

Sales assistant: 'This one has a green design with a shark. It must be the one she wants!'

Which one of the following sentences shows the mistake the sales assistant has made?

A Bree might now prefer a skateboard design with flowers.
B Even if the skateboard has a green design, it might not have a shark.
C There might be more than one design that is green with a shark.
D Bree might have seen the skateboard in the toy store.

22 In a full set of dominoes, each piece is unique. Each domino is made of two squares, with each square showing a 0 (blank), 1, 2, 3, 4, 5 or 6. There is a domino for every possible combination of those numbers, including doubles. For instance, there is a domino that has two blank squares on it, a domino that has a blank square and a one, all the way up to the domino that has two sixes on it.

How many dominoes are there in a set?

A 28   B 42   C 49   D 56

23 Five towns in a region are arranged like the four points of a diamond with one town in the middle.

It is known that:
• Town A is further north than Town C
• Town D is further south than Town C
• Town B is further east than Town E.

Which is the only map that could be the correct map of the region?

A   ● E
   D● ● B ● A
       ● C

B   ● A
   B● ● C ● E
       ● D

C   ● A
   E● ● B ● C
       ● D

D   ● A
   D● ● E ● B
       ● C

24 An architect has suggested that, instead of pulling down the old town hall building, it should be turned into a cinema and live-music venue.

Which one of these statements, if true, best supports the architect's claim?

A A developer wants to demolish the town hall and build an apartment block.
B The town currently has no venue for film or music.
C A petition from local residents called for the site to become a shopping mall.
D The architect's plan also includes a rooftop restaurant.

25 Gurbaj wants to make as many muffins as he can with the ingredients he has at home. He has found a recipe that uses 2 eggs, 125 g of butter, 180 g of sugar, 250 g of flour and 125 mL of milk.

At home he has a dozen eggs, 375 g of butter, 1 kg of sugar, 800 g of flour and 1 L of milk.

If he makes as many batches of muffins as he can, how much sugar will he have left over?

A 540 g

B 460 g

C 100 g

D 0 g

26 Yusaf's teacher wanted to rearrange the classroom. He decided to allow students to help him decide what to do in the back corner. Students could vote for a computer corner, a reading corner with beanbags or a science centre. Everyone had to cast two votes but they could not vote for the same idea twice. An idea would only win if everyone voted for it. If this did not happen then the teacher would make the final decision himself. Each idea received at least one vote.

Knowing one of the following would allow us to know the result of the vote. Which one is it?

A Computer corner was the most popular vote.

B Only two people voted for a science centre.

C Every student voted for either science centre or reading corner, or both.

D No student voted for both computer corner and science centre.

27 Virat is learning to juggle five balls. He has one yellow ball, two green balls and two red balls. After a while he decides to drop two and return to practising juggling three balls only.

He only has two colours left in his hands. What is **not** possible?

A Virat didn't drop the yellow ball.

B Virat dropped two differently coloured balls.

C Virat dropped the yellow ball.

D Virat dropped a green and a red ball.

28 The view of a single-storey building is shown below:

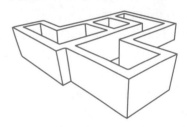

Which of the following diagrams could be the floor plan for this building?

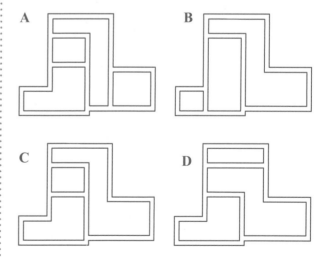

29 A street performer in front of a crowd sat at a table with five overturned cups in front of him. He put a ball underneath the cup furthest to the crowd's right. He then rearranged the cups so quickly that no one could follow them. He said to the crowd:

- none of the cups are in the same place as they were
- the cup that started on your far left is now at your far right
- the cups that started third and fourth from your left are still next to each other
- the cups that started second and third from your left are now separated by two other cups
- the ball is not in the middle cup.

Underneath which cup is the ball?

A first on the left

B second from the left

C third from the left

D fourth from the left

30 Locky's singing teacher said: 'Everybody who will pass the singing exam practises for at least 20 minutes, four times a week.'

Locky: 'I'm sure to pass the exam. I practise for 20 minutes, four times a week.'

Which of these sentences shows the mistake Locky has made?

A Practising for the required amount of time does not guarantee a pass in the exam.

B The teacher is talking about a different grade level.

C Someone else might practise for more than 20 minutes, four times a week.

D It is better to practise in a group than alone.

READING **Test 1**
Page 1

1 B 2 A 3 D 4 C 5 C 6 D 7 C 8 D 9 A
10 B 11 C 12 D 13 A 14 C 15 G 16 B
17 F 18 A 19 D 20 B 21 C 22 A 23 B
24 C 25 D

1 This is a narrative text that features talking animals in a fantasy setting. The text contains witty dialogue, absurd situations and silly riddles. This makes it amusing and entertaining. A is incorrect because the text does not contain any informative material. C is incorrect because, although the animals and the Hatter are strangers to Alice, there is no sense of danger. D is incorrect because the text does not raise any animal rights issues.

2 Alice sat down because the table was large, it had many places set and the others were all crowded together at one end. Alice's words in paragraph two indicate she thought it was expected that more people would come along and sit at the table. B is incorrect because she was not invited to join the others. C is incorrect because there was no wine on the table. D is incorrect because the riddles began **after** she sat down.

3 'Severity' means the act of being strict or harsh. Alice is speaking severely because she doesn't like people making personal comments about her hair; she thinks it shows bad manners. Alice's words follow on directly from the Hatter's comment on her hair. A is incorrect as there is nothing to imply Alice doesn't want to get her hair cut. B is incorrect because she is angry at being offered wine (not tea) when there isn't any. C is incorrect because, even though she may well be feeling embarrassed that she sat without being invited, this does not relate to the sentence.

4 The Hatter asks the question right after Alice reprimands him for his rudeness. 'The Hatter opened his eyes very wide on hearing this; but all he *said* was, "Why is a raven like a writing-desk?"' This had the effect of changing the subject away from his rudeness to the matter of the riddle. A is incorrect because Alice was glad they'd begun asking riddles and thought she would have some fun. B is incorrect because the tea party continued uninterrupted after the riddle was asked. D is incorrect because the Dormouse stayed asleep until later, when the Hatter poured tea on its nose.

5 Alice thinks the Hatter's behaviour is puzzling and finds him hard to understand: 'Alice felt dreadfully puzzled. The Hatter's remark seemed to have no sort of meaning in it, and yet it was certainly English.' A is incorrect because the Hatter did not encourage her to join them; instead he teased her with his unanswerable riddle and bizarre conversations. B is incorrect because, although the Hatter talks nonsense, his thoughts are not drifting uncontrollably. Instead, he plays with words cleverly and returns to his riddle at the end of the passage. D is incorrect because Alice thinks the Hatter is hard to understand so he is not well spoken and his conversation jumps around seemingly randomly, rather than being rational and well thought out.

6 The March Hare and the Hatter think it is normal for a watch to show the date and not the time. This—among other things—shows the reader that the text takes place in an odd fantasy world that differs from our own. A is incorrect because, even though the watch isn't working, this is only because it is showing the wrong date. B is incorrect because there is nothing to suggest time itself is standing still; the events in the passage progress as if time is flowing normally. C is incorrect because Alice does indeed understand what the Hatter is saying; however, his words do not make sense in the context of the real world.

7 The poem is called 'Suppose', which means to think or consider something. The poet is inviting the reader to think carefully about

what she has to say. A is incorrect because, although the word 'suppose' is repeated in the first sentence, it is not introducing the poem's key message. B is incorrect because there is nothing in the title itself to suggest the poem was written a long time ago. D is incorrect because the title suits the poem's content and the word 'suppose' is repeated throughout.

8 The poem discusses the things that can go wrong in life, including broken toys, getting caught in the rain, and general hardship and difficulties. A is incorrect because it doesn't discuss whether girls and boys should have different toys; indeed it takes this for granted because it was written a long time ago when attitudes were different. B is incorrect because even though the poem may suggest the lessons learnt in childhood will help children when they grow, it is not openly discussing this. C is incorrect because, even though it is possible to read into the poem a message that children should have good manners, the poem is not openly discussing this.

9 The children in the poem are upset and saddened by the things that can go wrong in life and have not yet learnt to deal with life's many disappointments. For example, this can be seen in the line: 'Will it make it any easier / For you to sit and fret?' B is incorrect because there is no indication the children have been spoilt; rather their lives are somewhat difficult: 'Will it tire you less while walking / To say, "It isn't fair?"' C is incorrect because, although the girl has a red nose and red eyes, this isn't due to an illness, and the boy's tiredness is the result of too much walking, rather than a physical weakness. D is incorrect because the children are struggling with the many small problems they encounter.

10 To 'make sunshine in the house' refers to making yourself and the other people in your home feel brighter and happier 'when there is none without', or during times of misfortunes. A is incorrect because it takes the passage too literally. The poet is talking about what will make the home feel happier, not literally brighter and warmer. C is incorrect because, although this is implied by the poem, it does not relate to the quotation.

D is incorrect because, even though this is mentioned in the poem, it comes after the relevant quotation and does not directly relate to it.

11 Throughout the poem, the poet points out the many things that can go wrong in life. She goes on to demonstrate that it is people's attitudes that matter. They can be happier and wiser if they make the best of things, rather than complaining about misfortune. The message is summarised in the last lines: 'And isn't it, my boy or girl, / The wisest, bravest plan, / Whatever comes, or doesn't come, / To do the best you can?' A is incorrect because, although the poem discusses the many things that can go wrong, it is by no means negative or defeatist in its tone. B is incorrect because there is no discussion of safety issues. D is incorrect because the issues affecting girls and boys are discussed separately, and there is no suggestion that this approach is wrong and that the different sexes should be treated equally.

12 In the previous sentence, the writer says the schoolgirls set off on an excursion to Hanging Rock. This sentence provides additional information about the site: 'This is a real location, in the Macedon Ranges north of Melbourne.' This emphasises it is a real place, rather than a fictional one, and describes where it is located.

13 In the previous sentence, the writer says the students and teachers experience bizarre events. This sentence provides an example of one such event: 'For example, all the teachers' watches stop working at the exact same time.' The sentence that follows identifies the time at which this happened.

14 In the previous sentence, the writer is describing the peculiar way in which three of the four girls behaved on the walk. This sentence shows what this fourth girl did in response and how her attempts were received: 'She tried to stop them but was completely ignored.' The sentence that follows describes how the fourth girl eventually made her way back to the picnic site but the other three did not.

15 In the previous sentence, the writer says the police searched for the missing girls. This sentence shows the results of that search: 'One girl was eventually found, unconscious and near to death.' The sentence that follows provides more details about the girl that was found.

16 In the previous sentence, the writer says fans of the film have tried to solve the mystery. This sentence shows how they did this: 'They flocked to libraries searching for news articles and police reports.' The sentence that follows provides more information about fans trying to solve the mystery and the odd solutions that some people have come up with.

17 In the previous sentence, the writer says that many people were convinced the story was real. This sentence shows why they may have thought this: 'This might be because the novel was written as if it were relating historical fact, when in fact it wasn't.' The sentence that follows adds more information about the issue.

Note: The unused sentence is E.

18 This is an extract from a novel, which is fictional. The creature described is purely a product of the writer's imagination. B is incorrect because this extract is an early description of a platypus. C is incorrect because, although hoop snakes most likely don't exist, the writer raises questions that suggest they might. D is incorrect because thylacines definitely once existed and the issue in this extract is whether they are really extinct or not.

19 The writer talks about the thylacines, which are believed to be extinct. The factors that led to their extinction (that is, the death of the species) are outlined in the extract. A, B and C are incorrect because they do not talk about the survival of a species.

20 The writer goes into great detail, minutely describing the appearance of the platypus's head, body, tail and feet. He even goes so far as to provide measurements. A, C and D are incorrect because they provide far less detailed descriptions than those contained in B.

21 The writer states that zoologists do not believe hoop snakes exist because the creatures are physically unable to move in the way that has been claimed: 'They point out that rolling is an unnatural way for snakes to travel: their muscles and bones simply are not made that way.' A is incorrect because the Hound of the Baskervilles is described as being unusually large, which is not impossible. B and D are incorrect because they describe animals that really exist and so are not physically impossible.

22 The writer uses expressions such as 'raised the hair upon their heads', 'blazing eyes and dripping jaws' and 'shrieked with fear'. This type of language evokes a sense of fear and danger. B, C and D are incorrect because these extracts do not use the sort of language that creates a frightening atmosphere. Instead they are more factual and/or conversational.

23 The writer is telling us about the discovery of a real new species; not a rumoured, extinct or fictional animal. The animal is the platypus, which amazed early scientists because they had never seen anything like it before. The extract was written in 1798, in the very early days of European settlement. The minute detail of the description and the way the animal is seen as a combination of different animal types reflects the sense of wonder that the discovery aroused. A is incorrect because this extract describes terror rather than a sense of wonder. C is incorrect because it does not deal with a genuine new species, as the writer states that hoop snakes probably don't really exist. D is incorrect because it is talking about an extinct species, not a newly discovered species.

24 The writer states that many sightings of hoop snakes were made following a series of Pecos Bill cowboy stories. This shows that people can be overly influenced by popular culture, so much so that they may believe something exists simply because they read about it. A is incorrect because it is an extract from a novel. B is incorrect because it is primarily a description of a newly discovered animal species. D is incorrect because there is no suggestion that the people who claim to have seen thylacines are doing so because they were influenced by popular culture.

25 The writer mentions that human activity contributed to making thylacines extinct. More specifically, it states that farmers slaughtered the animals because they thought thylacines killed their livestock. Climate change is also mentioned as a cause of the extinction. It is generally accepted that humans are responsible for the accelerated climate change that we have experienced in recent centuries. A, B and C are incorrect because the issue is not raised in these texts.

READING Test 2

Page 8

1 A 2 B 3 D 4 C 5 B 6 D 7 D 8 C 9 B
10 A 11 B 12 D 13 B 14 G 15 A 16 F
17 E 18 D 19 C 20 A 21 B 22 C 23 D
24 A 25 B

1 Tim talks to the tiger-skin rug because he feels some sense of the fact that the rug was once a living animal. B is incorrect because Tim is not frightened of Hercules and is not trying to convince the hero that the rug is alive: 'It's not dangerous, it's just a rug.' C is incorrect because there is nothing to suggest that Tim cannot distinguish fantasy from reality; if that were the case, he would not be trying to convince Hercules the rug was not alive. D is incorrect because Tim does not imagine the rug is talking back to him; neither is he wondering why it has not replied.

2 The reference to the monster from Greek mythology shows that Hercules is trying to relive his past glories. He refers to his past victory in an attempt to intimidate and frighten the tiger skin, which he believes to be alive: 'I've beaten mightier foes than you. Even the Lion of Nemea, the most fearsome beast in the world'. A is incorrect because the passage is not frightening, it is amusing. C is incorrect because the author is making the reference to provide an insight into Hercules' character, rather than to display her knowledge of mythology. D is incorrect because there is no description as to what the Nemean Lion looked like, nor anything to imply their appearances are being compared.

3 Hercules is a figure from Greek mythology. His unusual concerns for Tim's safety, such as the fear that Tim might have arrows fired at him on the way to school, show that the world he comes from is more dangerous than our own. A is incorrect because there is nothing to suggest Tim comes from a dangerous neighbourhood and indeed it is unlikely he lives in a place where arrows would be fired at him on the way to school. B is incorrect because Hercules makes no mention of a powerful enemy; his concerns seem to be more generalised. C is incorrect because the issue is not mentioned in this passage and there is nothing to make the reader infer this.

4 To commiserate with somebody means to express pity or sympathy for their misfortune or condition. Hercules thought Tim believed the tiger-skin rug was actually a tiger: this is despite Tim telling him repeatedly it wasn't. 'He gave Tim a commiserative glance. 'I hate to say this, my friend, but you were wrong. This is not a man-eater after all! It's just a skin.' A is incorrect because Hercules thought the tiger was dangerous and he was clearly trying to defeat it. B is incorrect because Hercules was totally unaware of what Tim was actually worried about, which was indeed the rug getting damaged. D is incorrect because, although it is true, this is not directly connected to the phrase in question.

5 Tim is hardworking and kind. He is hardworking because he is putting a lot of effort into cleaning a rug. He is kind because of the way he speaks to the rug, as if it were a live animal, and in the way he didn't ridicule Hercules for his mistake. A is incorrect because Tim is clearly not frightened of the rug. C is incorrect because Tim patiently tries to explain that it is not a real tiger and he only argues because he has to stop Hercules from destroying it. D is incorrect because he can see reality for what it is, despite Hercules thinking otherwise.

6 Hercules is loving but overprotective. He charges in to protect Tim from what he wrongly considers to be a danger: 'Do not fear, Tim Baker, the mighty Hercules will save you!' He also wants to protect Tim from another non-existent danger, that of being shot with arrows on the way to school: 'You need all the help you can get'. A is incorrect because Hercules shows by his actions and speech that he is the exact opposite. B is incorrect because, although Hercules becomes irritated and angry, it is with the tiger-skin rug, not with Tim. C is incorrect because, although Hercules is loving, he doesn't really respect Tim. He disregards what Tim is trying to tell him about the rug and the cloak, and sees him mostly as someone to protect.

7   Lorelei is the name of the beautiful woman. She is described as the 'loveliest maiden', who 'sings a song'. Her identity is made clear in the final lines: 'And with her singing / The Lorelei did this'. A is incorrect because the name of the river is the Rhine: 'the Rhine is flowing quietly by'. B and C are incorrect because the boat and the boatman are never named.

8   The narrator is feeling sad because he is recalling an ancient tale: 'I am so sad; / There's a tale from ancient times / That I can't get out of my mind'. The tale is one of tragedy. A is incorrect because the narrator himself is not trying to reach the maiden, rather he is telling the story of a boatman. B is incorrect because, although 'The air is cool and the twilight is falling', he isn't feeling sad about that; instead the description is peaceful and pleasant. D is incorrect because it is not the narrator's boat that is capsizing, rather he is telling the story of an unfortunate boatman.

9   An 'unrestrained' emotion is an extreme or intense one, and 'woe' refers to sadness. The song made the boatman feel intensely sad: 'A song with a peculiar, / Powerful melody.' It seizes upon the boatman in his small boat 'With unrestrained woe'. A is incorrect because the boatman wasn't worried about sinking; instead he was totally focused on the lovely maiden. C is incorrect because the maiden was not calling out a warning, rather she was luring the boatman to his doom. D is incorrect because the boat only broke and crashed when it hit the rocky shoals.

10   The boat sinks because the boatman is not looking where he is going: 'He does not look below the rocky shoals; / He only looks up at the heights.' B is incorrect because, although the boat is described as being small, there is nothing to suggest it is unsafe. C is incorrect because there is nothing to suggest the water was rough. D is incorrect because, although the boatman was strongly affected by the singing, it was his failure to look where he was going that caused the crash.

11   The Lorelei is deliberately luring the boatman to his doom. She is showing off her beauty while she sings a powerful and enchanting song. The fact that she acted deliberately can be seen in the final lines: 'And with her singing / The Lorelei did this'. A is incorrect because it can be inferred in the poem that she is putting on a performance for the sake of the boatman. C is incorrect because the song is described as 'peculiar' and 'powerful', rather than mournful, and there is nothing to suggest she is foretelling his future. D is incorrect because there is nothing to suggest the boatman is daydreaming or hallucinating.

12   In the previous sentence, the writer says some places are so special they are of global significance. This sentence explains what it means for something to be of global significance: 'They matter to all of humanity, not only to the people who live there.' The sentence that follows explains what happens to such places: they are put on the World Heritage List.

13   In the previous sentence, the writer says only certain countries can nominate places for the list. This sentence provides more information about what happens when a country nominates a place: 'Even if placed on the list, each site is still owned by the country it is located in.' The sentence that follows continues talking about the types of places that can be nominated.

14   The previous sentences talk about the criteria for a place to be considered of natural significance. This sentence provides an example of one such place: 'Australia's Great Barrier Reef is such an example.' The sentence that follows contains information about the Great Barrier Reef.

15 In the previous sentence, the writer says cultural sites carry different criteria. This sentence is one such criterion: 'A cultural site may represent a masterpiece of human creative genius.' The sentences that follow provide other types of criteria.

16 In the previous sentence, the writer says some sites have both cultural and natural significance. This sentence provides an example: 'For example, Uluru is naturally occurring but has great cultural significance.' The sentence that follows contains more information about Uluru.

17 In the previous sentences, the writer says some places are so in danger they need to be placed on a special list. This sentence looks at some of the reasons why the sites may be in danger: 'Examples of threats include wars, pollution, and natural disasters.' It concludes the passage.

Note: The unused sentence is C.

18 This extract identifies multiple subsidiary (additional) benefits of learning to play an instrument. They include self-discipline, commitment, improved brain function and improved motor skills. A is incorrect because the only subsidiary benefit that can be inferred from this extract is family togetherness. B is incorrect because the only subsidiary benefit that can be inferred is social acceptance. C is incorrect because the only subsidiary benefit that can be inferred is stress release.

19 This extract is a recount by a person who turns to music when they feel upset or stressed, thus treating it as a form of therapy: 'Whenever something worries or upsets me, I lose myself completely in my music'. A is incorrect because the issue is not raised or implied. B is incorrect because here music is seen as a social duty, which is far from being a type of therapy or a stress release. D is incorrect because, although it outlines many benefits of learning an instrument, no type of therapy is mentioned.

20 This extract describes a family singing and playing piano together, and mentions they had been doing it for a very long time: 'it had become a household custom'. The affectionate way music is described suggests that it contributes to family togetherness in that household. B is incorrect because the characters are not related and practising piano is seen as something to be done 'in nobody's way', rather than as a family group. C and D are incorrect as there is no mention of music bringing people together.

21 This extract hints that, at the time the novel was written, ladies were expected to be accomplished piano players: 'I am very glad to hear such a good account of her'; 'I often tell young ladies that no excellence in music is to be acquired without constant practice.' A is incorrect because the characters are singing and playing within the home and for each other, not in broader society. C is incorrect because it describes personal, not social, reasons for playing. D is incorrect because it mainly focuses on the benefits to a child's education and learning.

22 This extract describes how the narrator initially had a negative attitude towards learning—'At first, I hated it'—but as they grew older their opinion changed: 'However, now I'm so grateful.' A is incorrect because the attitude of the family members towards music did not change over time: 'the girls never grew too old for that familiar lullaby'. B is incorrect because the only person's attitude we are given is that of Lady Catherine, which does not change. D is incorrect because it provides a discussion about the benefits of learning music, rather than an insight into children's attitudes.

23 This extract mentions specific jargon in relation to music lessons, including 'fine motor skills' and 'spatial awareness'. A, B and C are incorrect because they are conversational rather than technical and do not make use of jargon related to learning to play a musical instrument.

24 This extract describes the different levels of musical skills within the family: only Beth can play the piano well, and while Meg and the mother are good singers, Amy 'chirped like a cricket' and Jo could not hit the right note. B is incorrect because it only discusses the need for one person to practise. C is incorrect because the narrator is only talking about their own abilities. D is incorrect because there is no comparison between different people's abilities.

25 This extract features a character who is offering the use of her piano for another person to practise on because they do not have their own. A is incorrect because the family has their own piano. C is incorrect because the narrator practised 'on our piano'. D is incorrect because it is an analysis about the benefits of learning to play and the issue does not arise.

READING Test 3

Page 15

> 1 A 2 C 3 D 4 B 5 D 6 C 7 A 8 C 9 B
> 10 D 11 B 12 B 13 E 14 A 15 F 16 G
> 17 C 18 C 19 D 20 A 21 D 22 C 23 B
> 24 A 25 B

1 Tom insisted on painting the fence himself because he was trying to manipulate Ben into wanting to do it by making it seem unobtainable. B is incorrect because, even though Tom expressed such concerns, he did not mean it and was trying to influence Ben. C is incorrect because, although Aunt Polly did indeed tell him to paint the fence, this was not his motivation. D is incorrect because he did not enjoy painting fences; instead he was trying to manipulate other boys into doing it for him.

2 Tom thought that if something is hard to obtain, others would want it. This is why he pretended to be reluctant when Ben wanted to paint the fence. A is incorrect because Tom didn't want to paint the fence; he would rather play or swim. B is incorrect because Tom thought painting was hard work and so he tricked the other boys into doing it for him. D is incorrect because, although Tom fussed about the importance of painting properly, it was only to entice others to do it.

3 Tom had convinced Ben that painting the fence was desirable. He did this by pretending he actually wanted to do it, rather than admitting he was forced to: '…"Well, I don't see why I oughtn't to like it. Does a boy get a chance to whitewash a fence every day?" That put the thing in a new light.' A is incorrect because Ben didn't feel sorry for Tom, instead he was teasing him because he had to work. B is incorrect because Ben had no connection to Aunt Polly (she is Tom's

aunty), and had no interest in impressing her. C is incorrect because Ben only gave up his apple in order to get the chance to paint; at first he only offered the core but then had to increase his offer.

4 Another word for 'alacrity' in this context is eagerness. Its meaning is hinted at in this sentence—'Tom gave up the brush with reluctance in his face, but alacrity in his heart'—and in the text that leads up to it. Tom pretended to be reluctant to let Ben paint but it was what he was working towards all along, and he was keen and eager to hand it over. A and C are incorrect because Tom felt happy to let someone else paint; he was not angry or miserable. D is incorrect because Tom was not the slightest bit confused; instead he had deliberately manipulated Ben into doing his work.

5 Tom Sawyer is lazy and cunning. He does not want to paint the fence and so he tricks other boys into doing the work for him: 'He had had a nice, good, idle time all the while—plenty of company—and the fence had three coats of whitewash on it!' A is incorrect because Tom is getting others to do his work for him. Therefore he is not hardworking. B is incorrect because, although he is pretending to be generous in allowing others to paint, he is actually profiting from them. C is incorrect because Tom is deliberately disobeying Aunt Polly, who told him to paint the fence.

6 The message of the extract is summed up in the last line: 'Work consists of whatever a body is obliged to do, and that Play consists of whatever a body is not obliged to do.' Tom was obliged to do the chore but the other boys were not, so they saw the task as play rather than work. A is incorrect because painting a fence is hard; Tom saw it as work but managed to convince the others that it was play. B is incorrect because Tom is not being paid to paint the fence; rather it is a chore imposed by his Aunt. D is incorrect because the author makes it clear there is a difference.

7 The poem is about nature. The poem's narrator is sitting outdoors in a grove (a small group of trees), watching the birds and animals, and listening to the sounds of nature. B is incorrect because the poem does not mention the sound of a battle and there is nothing to infer one is taking place. C is incorrect because the poem does not mention music and there is nothing to infer someone is playing music. D is incorrect because it is based on a misunderstanding of what is meant by notes.

8 The narrator is enjoying nature but is filled with sadness when he thinks about humanity: 'And much it grieved my heart to think / What man has made of man'. He links the human soul to nature but is upset that people do not treat each other well. A is incorrect because the poet describes nature in a way that captures its beauty and majesty. B is incorrect because the thought of humanity saddens him, while being among nature gives him a sense of ease and delight. D is incorrect because there is nothing in the poem to infer he has lost a loved one; instead he grieves because of the way humans treat each other.

9 The narrator describes plants and animals in a way that portrays them as being happy and grateful to be alive. When describing plants and birds, the language used includes 'Enjoys the air it breathes', 'It seemed a thrill of pleasure' and 'that there was pleasure there'. A is incorrect because nature is shown as being beautiful and uplifting; there is nothing menacing or dangerous in the description. C and D are incorrect because the narrator does not offer any insights into how he thinks nature feels about humanity.

10 The poem ends on a sombre and sad note. Although the narrator is seeking healing from nature, he is still feeling sad about the way humans treat each other: 'Have I not reason to lament / What man has made of man?' To lament means to express sorrow or grief. A is incorrect because, although he finds joy and optimism in nature, he is nevertheless saddened that humans are not the same. B is incorrect because there is nothing to suggest bitterness or anger in the poem; rather it feels more like disappointment. C is incorrect because the narrator is very sure of what he is saying: there is no sense of uncertainty or confusion, even though the poem ends with a question.

11 The poem's mood is quiet and reflective, as summarised in the lines: 'In that sweet mood when pleasant thoughts / Bring sad thoughts to the mind.' The narrator is looking at the beauty of nature and its joy of life, while reflecting that humans cause each other misery. A is incorrect, as the natural setting gives the poem a sense of calm. C is incorrect as there is nothing menacing or dangerous about the poem. D is incorrect because, although the narrator is feeling sad about humanity, he still enjoys the sights of nature and imagines the joy experienced by the plants and birds.

12 In the previous sentence, the writer says the energy market is changing. This sentence shows why it is changing: 'This reflects increasing concern about the state of the environment and the need for sustainability.' The sentence that follows introduces the question of how it is changing.

13 In the previous sentence, the writer explains what non-renewable resources are. This sentence provides information about how they were formed: 'These are mostly fossil fuels, which were formed deep inside the Earth's crust.' The sentence that follows gives more details about the process.

14 In the previous sentence, the writer says we are using fossil fuels too quickly. This sentence shows what the consequences are: 'This means they will eventually run out.' The sentence that follows gives an indication of how long it would take for new fossil fuels to be created.

15 In the previous sentence, the writer explains what renewable resources are. This sentence explains in more detail what renewable means: 'They replace themselves naturally over time.' The sentence that follows gives examples of two renewable resources.

16 In the previous sentence, the writer says photovoltaic cells can be used to create electricity. This sentence explains how this happens: 'Made from silicon and other materials, these transform sunlight into electricity.' The sentence that follows gives an indication of where the cells are used.

17 In the previous sentence, the writer says turbines use wind power to generate electricity. This sentence shows how this works: 'As the wind blows, the blades turn, feeding an electric generator.' The sentence that follows provides information about where wind turbines are situated.

Note: The unused sentence is D.

18 This extract is a personal recount containing childhood recollections. The writer, who is now an adult, expressly recalls having headlice as a child. A is incorrect because the child is still a child in this narrative. B is incorrect because it is an extract from a diary written by an adult about his experience as an adult, not as a child. D is incorrect because it is a report that provides information about lice and treatments.

19 This extract is an information report explaining the difference between lice and nits. A and B are incorrect because they only talk about lice; they do not mention nits at all. C is incorrect because, although the writer mentions both nits and lice, no attempt is made to identify the difference between them.

20 This extract is a passage from a narrative featuring Mike's attempts to get rid of his headlice. He hangs upside down from the clothesline hoping that gravity will do the trick, but this fails. There is also a suggestion he is going to try something else (involving his dog) that will also fail. B is incorrect because the writer's wife successfully treats him for nits. C is incorrect because the writer had successfully been treated for nits as a child and we can presume will be treated again. D is incorrect because it provides information, rather than describes someone's experiences.

21 This extract looks at the consequences of not treating headlice. It states that, although it won't lead to disease, the condition is uncomfortable and unpleasant. It also warns that failure to treat the condition will allow the headlice to rapidly reproduce. A is incorrect because the consequences of Mike's actions are not mentioned in this passage. He is worried that his head might be shaved but this is just a fear, not a consequence. B and C are incorrect because the headlice were treated successfully and the writers did not discuss what might have otherwise happened.

22 In this extract, the writer mentions not feeling itchy until they discovered they had lice. The inference is that it is possible to have headlice without feeling itchy. A is incorrect because Mike's head is itchy. B is incorrect because the writer stated that he had been feeling itchy. D is incorrect because the issue does not come up.

23 This extract is a passage from a diary written in 1669. The writer is referring to lice hundreds of years ago, which shows they've been around for a very long time. A is incorrect because it is set in the modern day and makes no reference to the past. C is incorrect because it is set in the modern day. Even though the writer refers to their childhood, this is only the recent past. D is incorrect because it only deals with the present-day occurrence and treatment of headlice.

24 This extract is from a novel that uses humour to deliver its message. Humour can be found in the unusual ways in which Mike tries to solve his problem and in his amusing explanations as to why they didn't work. For example, the lice were wearing 'anti-gravity boots'. B is incorrect as the writing style is down to earth and serious. C is incorrect because, although it is written in a friendly and conversational style, it is not humorous. D is incorrect because it provides factual information and makes no attempt at humour.

25 In this extract the writer of the diary was not only talking about lice, he was also concerned with money (his 'accounts'). He talks about being otherwise well and feels content when the lice are removed, showing that he took the whole thing in his stride. A is incorrect because Mike is going to extraordinary lengths to rid himself of what he sees as a major problem. C is incorrect because the writer does not mention any other challenges or problems they have faced apart from headlice. D is incorrect because it simply provides factual information about nits, lice and their treatment.

MATHEMATICAL REASONING Test 1   Page 21

1 C 2 B 3 C 4 C 5 A 6 A 7 B 8 E 9 E
10 B 11 C 12 C 13 D 14 A 15 D 16 A
17 B 18 B 19 E 20 D 21 C 22 D 23 B
24 B 25 C 26 D 27 E 28 B 29 A 30 E
31 A 32 C 33 A 34 B 35 E

1 86 is 14 from 100, 111 is 11 from 100, 448 is 48 from 400, 582 is 18 from 600 and 713 is 13 from 700. This means 448 changes the most.

2 Look for two numbers that add to 36, where one is twice the other. The two numbers are 12 and 24. This means the shorter piece is 12 cm.

3 $24 \div 8 = 3$ and $X = 3 \times 5 = 15$. Here is the completed puzzle:

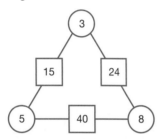

4 There are 12 units between 120 and 156. As $156 - 120$ is 36, and $36 \div 12 = 3$, each unit represents 3. The arrow is 4 units from 120. As $4 \times 3 = 12$ and $120 + 12 = 132$, the arrow is pointing to 132.

5 The girl's ages add to 18 and have a difference of 12. The ages now are 15 and 3. This means Charlotte is 3 years old and in 4 years she will be 7 years old.

6 The answer is 7 because it is made up of four 25-cent coins, one 5-cent coin and two 1-cent coins.

7 In the first fold, I is behind the H. After the second fold, E and L are also behind the H.

8 Here is the order of students using letters for the named students and numbers representing the other students: L 5 G ? P 8 E.
As $1 + 5 + 1 + 1 + 8 + 1 = 17$, and $24 - 17 = 7$, there are 7 students between Peyton and Grace.

9 There are 12 edges on a cube. As $12 \times 5 = 60$, the cube is made using 60 cm of wire.

10 The three squares are A4, E8, H2. Here is Jerome's final grid:

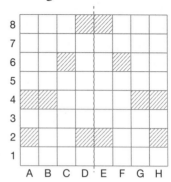

11 1 has 1 factor: 1; 2 has 2: 1, 2; 3 has 2: 1, 3; 4 has 3: 1, 2, 4; 6 has 4: 1, 2, 3, 6; and 8 has 4: 1, 2, 4, 8. This means 3 and 6 have a total of 6 factors.

12 As $4 - 1 - 2 = 1$, Isabella has kept one of the four pieces. This means she has one-quarter of the cake. She then gave half of her quarter to her mother. This means she gave one-eighth of the cake to her mother.

13 The correct sum is shown below. A starting point would have been the letter U — this could only have been a two (2).

MU	32
× 4	× 4
CU8	128

14 From 7:30 pm to 7:45 pm is 15 min. From 7:45 pm to 6:45 am the next morning is 11 h. This is a total of 11 h 15 min.

15 Mitchell will need to add two rows of 5, two rows of 6 and two rows of 7. This means he will need to add 36 more cubes.

16 Each number has 4 digits. The first digit is increasing by 1, the second decreasing by 2, the third increasing by 2 and the fourth increasing by 1. The next number will be 7098.

17 There are 12 small rectangles. Six of the 12 rectangles are already shaded. $\frac{1}{4}$ of 12 is $12 \div 4 = 3$. $\frac{3}{4}$ of 12 is $3 \times 3 = 9$. This means 9 rectangles need to be shaded. As $9 - 6 = 3$, there need to be another 3 rectangles shaded.

18 Christopher scored full marks 4 times, which gave him $40. He didn't get full marks 6 times, which meant he had to pay his parents $30 and so he was left with $10. If this was a bit hard for you, testing the answers would have given you the correct response.

19 Work in reverse with inverse operations. Start with Clare's answer of 16. 16 − 10 + 4 − 8 = 2. Clare started with 2.

20 The sum of the length and width of the rectangle is 15 cm. This means the dimensions are 10 cm and 5 cm. As 10 × 5 = 50, the area is 50 cm².

21 Each interval on the ruler is 2 cm. Krystal's height is 56 − 16 = 40 cm, and Erin's height is 34 − 20 = 14 cm. The difference is 40 − 14 = 26 cm.

22 In Bag 1, 6 + 9 + 1 = 16.
In Bag 2, 10 + 7 + 7 = 24. As 24 + 16 = 40, there is a total of 40 balls in the bags.

23 As 60 ÷ 10 = 6 and 6 × 100 = 600, our car can travel 600 km on one tank of petrol. This means we fill up three times: after 600 km, 1200 km and 1800 km.

24 To work this out you can start by crossing out symbols that appear on both sides of the scale because they balance each other out. A star on the left and another from the right will balance each other out. Next a cylinder on each side will be crossed out. One cube remains on the left and 3 stars remain on the right; therefore 1 cube = 3 stars in weight. Dividing 6 kg by 3 gives you the weight of 1 star.

25 There is 1000 g in 1 kg. Two lots of 1.5 kg is 3 kg. Britt should buy 2 bags of 1.5 kg and 2 bags of 500 g.
As 2 × \$6 plus 2 × \$2.50 = \$12 + \$5 = \$17, the smallest amount is \$17.

26 Myles: There are 4 rows of 6 squares. Shading $\frac{1}{4}$ of the grid means shading a row of squares. This means there are 3 rows unshaded.
Pablo: Shading $\frac{2}{3}$ of the unshaded squares means shading 2 rows of squares. This means there are 6 squares unshaded.
Olivia: Shading $\frac{1}{2}$ of the unshaded squares means shading 3 squares. This means there are 3 squares unshaded.

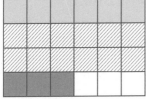

27 3 weeks is 21 days, and there are 30 days in June. As 21 − 5 = 16, and 30 − 16 = 14, Claire's birthday is 14 June.

28 As A, E, H, M, T, V and W have at least one line of symmetry, there are 7 letters.

29 The new rectangle is 8 units long and 2 units wide. As 8 + 8 + 2 + 2 = 20, the perimeter is 20 units.

30 There are 2 numbers less than 3, and 2 numbers greater than 4. This means it is equally likely. Statement 1 is not correct. The multiples of 3 are 3 and 6. The multiples of 2 are 2, 4 and 6. It is not more likely. Statement 2 is not correct. There are 3 factors of 4 (1, 2, 4) and there are 4 factors of 6 (1, 2, 3, 6). It is not equally likely. Statement 3 is not correct. None of the statements are correct.

31 This can be a difficult question but it is easier to work out if you sketch the answer.

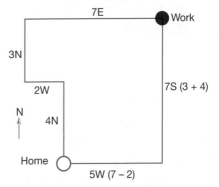

32 The factors of 6 are 1, 2, 3 and 6. 1 has no right angle, 2 has 4 right angles, 3 has 4 right angles and 6 has 6 right angles. As 0 + 4 + 4 + 6 = 14, there is a total of 14 right angles.

33 The shapes IV, V and VI made up the pattern shown below.

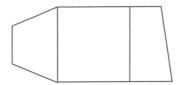

34 The 9 cubes in the centre of the bottom layer will not be painted, and neither will the centre cube in the second layer. This makes 10 without any blue paint on them. All the others have at least one side painted. Remember: If you are not sure, just guess instead of leaving the answer blank.

35 Sky (14 books) read twice as many as Joy (7). Claim 1 is correct. As Ben read 4 and Joy 7, the two students read a total of 11 books. This is the same number as Rae read (11). Claim 2 is correct. As $4 + 7 + 14 + 11 + 5 = 41$, the students read more than 40 books altogether. Claim 3 is correct. Claims 1, 2 and 3 are correct.

MATHEMATICAL REASONING Test 2 Page 27

1 E 2 D 3 B 4 E 5 C 6 D 7 E 8 B 9 D
10 C 11 E 12 A 13 A 14 E 15 D 16 B
17 A 18 E 19 D 20 C 21 A 22 E 23 E
24 E 25 D 26 E 27 C 28 A 29 C 30 B
31 E 32 D 33 E 34 A 35 D

1 As $10 + 11 + 6 = 27$, the sum of each row, column and diagonal is 27. Here is the final square:

10	5	12
11	9	7
6	13	8

The missing number is 8.

2 The number halfway is the middle, or average, of the two numbers. As $23 + 51 = 74$, and $74 \div 2 = 37$, the number is 37.

3 Start with James's answer and use the inverse operations. 14 plus 10 is 24. Halving this number gives 12. Now subtract 4 to get 8. James's original number was 8.

4 E has 4 right angles, T has 2, F has 3, H has 4 and L has 1. As $1 + 2 + 3 = 6$, the smallest possible total is 6 when L, T and F are chosen.

5 If one-fifth of the number is 10, then 50 is the number ($5 \times 10 = 50$).
Half of 50 is 25 ($50 \div 2 = 25$). This means the number sentence to be used is $10 \times 5 \div 2$.

6 The cube faces that will not be painted are the faces that cannot be seen if the shape was picked up and viewed from all directions. As $7 \times 6 = 42$, the 7 cubes have a total of 42 faces. In the shape there are 4 cube faces on the front and 4 on the back. There are 3 cube faces looking from the left and 3 from the right. There are 6 cube faces looking from the top and 6 from beneath. As $4 + 4 + 3 + 3 + 6 + 6 = 26$, there will be 26 cube faces that are painted. As $42 - 26 = 16$, there will be 16 cube faces not painted.

7 As $16 \div 2 = 8$, there are 8 lots of 2s in 16. Now, as multiplying 3 by 8 gives 24, Claire uses 24 red beads.

8 A triangle with 2 equal sides has 1 line of symmetry. A parallelogram has no lines of symmetry. A square has 4 lines of symmetry. As $1 + 0 + 4 = 5$, the total is 5 lines of symmetry.

9 From the sketch, the campsite is north-west.

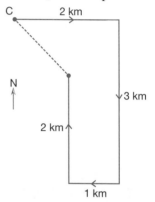

10 Col is 146 cm tall, and the shortest student is Don who is 139 cm tall. As $146 - 139 = 7$, Col is 7 cm taller. Claim 1 is not correct. Ela is the fifth tallest student. Claim 2 is not correct. Ada, Ben, Col and Flo are at least 144 cm tall. Claim 3 is correct.

11 From 0 to 20 there are 5 units. As $20 \div 5 = 4$, the number line is marked in 4s. This means $A = 12$, $C = 24$ and $B = 32$.
$A + C - B = 12 + 24 - 32$ which is $36 - 32 = 4$.

12 There are 60 minutes in an hour. From 11:54 am to midday is 6 minutes. To 1 pm is an hour and another 18 minutes to 1:18 pm. As $6 + 60 + 18 = 84$, the plumber was at the apartment for 84 minutes.

13 From 10 am to 1 pm is 3 hours with another 20 minutes meaning Allegra must pay for 4 hours of parking. As her first 2 hours are free, she pays for the last 2 hours.
As $7 + 3 = 10$ and $50 - 10 = 40$, Allegra should receive $40 in change.

14 A multiple of 3 and 5 is 15. This means that all multiples of 15 are multiples of 3 and 5. Abbie could have 15, 30 or 45 beads. But as $30 \div 7$ has a remainder of 2, Abbie has 30 beads.

15 As $5 \times 2 = 10$, then $Y = 10$. As $2 \times 4 = 8$, then $Z = 8$. As $Y \times Z = X$ and $10 \times 8 = 80$, the value of X is 80. Here is the completed diagram:

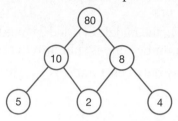

16 As $16 \div 4 = 4$ and $16 - 4 = 12$, Jannah had 12 chocolates remaining after Saturday. As $12 \div 2 = 6$ and $12 - 6 = 6$, Jannah had 6 chocolates remaining after Sunday. This means 6 chocolates were left in the box.

17 As $10 - 4 = 6$, there are 6 squares not shaded. Now, $\frac{2}{3}$ is the same as $\frac{4}{6}$, so Jen shades 4 out of the 6 squares. As $6 - 4 = 2$, there are eventually only 2 squares that remain unshaded.

18 As 12 plus 7 lots of 3 is $12 + 21 = 33$, he plans to complete 33 push-ups a week from today. (The sequence is 12, 15, 18, 21, 24, 27, 30, 33 …)

19 Here are some multiples of 5: 5, 10, 15, 20. There are 4 multiples of 5 less than 24. This means the principal chose 4 students.

20 To find out how many rolls of grass fit on the block of land, first divide the sides by the size of the grass. 32 divided by 4 is 8, so 8 rolls fit across. 16 divided by 2 is also 8, so 8 rolls fit along both sides. $8 \times 8 = 64$, so 64 rolls of grass fit on the land.

21 $48 + 35$ is $48 + 30 + 5 = 78 + 5 = 83$. Now, if $63 + \blacktriangle = 83$, then the missing number is $83 - 63 = 20$.

22 As $12 - 6 - 3 = 3$, there are 3 green balls in the bag. This means to choose a blue ball or a green ball is equally likely. Claim 1 is correct. There are 6 red balls and 3 blue balls. It is twice as likely that a red ball rather than a blue ball is chosen. Claim 2 is correct. After 3 red balls are removed there are 3 red balls, 3 blue balls and 3 green balls. To choose a red, blue or green ball is equally likely. Claim 3 is correct. Claims 1, 2 and 3 are correct.

23 $200 - 70$ is 130 and $130 - 40 = 90$. As $90 \div 3 = 30$, Josh spent $30 at the cinema. As $90 - 30 = 60$, Josh has $60 remaining on the card.

24 As $280 \div 2 = 140$ and $140 + 180 = 320$, Cleo now has 320 mL in Container B. As $400 - 320 = 80$, she needs another 80 mL to fill Container B.

25 As $410 - 235 = 175$, half of the peanut butter has a mass of 175 g. As $175 \times 2 = 350$, all the peanut butter has a mass of 350 g. As $410 - 350 = 60$, the empty jar has a mass of 60 g.

26 $20 = 7 + 5 + 8$, $21 = 12 + 7 + 2$, $19 = 12 + 7$ and $34 = 12 + 7 + 5 + 8 + 2$. However, 23 kg cannot be measured using the blocks.

27 As $5 \times 3 = 15$, each wall has an area of 15 m². As $15 \times 4 = 60$, the total area to be painted is 60 m². As $60 \div 6 = 10$, Trae will need 10 L.

28 Ellipse has 2 lines of symmetry, equilateral triangle 3, circle infinite, rectangle 2, parallelogram 0, isosceles triangle 1, pentagon 5 and octagon 8. This means 3 shapes have at least 4 lines of symmetry.

29 There are 31 days in October. A week after Tameka's birthday is Tuesday 1 November. This means 8 November and 15 November are also Tuesdays. As $15 + 2 = 17$, Caitlin's birthday is on a Thursday.

30 As $28 - 16 = 12$, the perimeter of the smaller square is 12 cm. As $12 \div 4 = 3$, the smaller square has a side length of 3 cm. As $3 \times 3 = 9$, the area of the smaller square is 9 cm².

31 This shape is impossible to form:

32 As $4 \times 3 = 12$, the rectangle covers 12 grid squares. As $48 \div 12 = 4$, each grid square has an area of 4 cm². This means that each side of a grid square is 2 cm. The large square has side lengths of 4 units which is 8 cm. As $8 \times 4 = 32$, the perimeter of the square is 32 cm.

33 Jeremiah can cut the rectangle in 3 different ways so that the two pieces are identical:

All statements can be true.

34 First there are 7 prisms arranged in the row. There are 3 more stacked at the start, 1 towards the end and 2 at the end. As $7 + 3 + 1 + 2 = 13$, there are 13 prisms.

35 Levi received 6 votes from 4P and 10 votes from 5K. Statement 1 is not correct. In Class 4P: 12 + 6 + 4 + 8 = 30. In Class 5K: 6 + 10 + 10 + 4 = 30. Statement 2 is correct. The total number of votes were: Aria (12 + 6 = 18), Levi (6 + 10 = 16), Jack (4 + 10 = 14), Isla (8 + 4 = 12). Isla received the least number of votes. Statement 3 is correct. Statements 2 and 3 are correct.

MATHEMATICAL REASONING Test 3 Page 32

1 D 2 D 3 C 4 D 5 A 6 E 7 D 8 D 9 E
10 E 11 D 12 B 13 D 14 E 15 C 16 E
17 E 18 E 19 D 20 B 21 B 22 D 23 C
24 D 25 E 26 B 27 D 28 D 29 E 30 C
31 A 32 E 33 E 34 C 35 B

1 Jemima can be given a 5-cent coin, 10-cent coin, 50-cent coin and two $2 coins. This means she could receive 5 coins.

2 $1 \times 2 \times 3 \times 4 = 24$. Two of the numbers are 2 and 4.

3 As 4000 − 80 is 3200, the difference is 3200.

4 Half of 48 is 24. This means the larger number is 24 more than 50 and the smaller is 24 less than 50. As 50 + 24 = 74, the larger number is 74.

5 The dotted line already passes through the squares B2 and G7. Also, H5 reflects to E8 already. This means Eve only needs to shade 1 square which is C4.

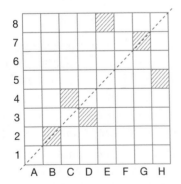

6 As 80 − 20 = 60 and 60 × 12 = 720, there are 720 remaining at 10 am. There are 5 hours between 10 am and 3 pm. As 100 × 5 = 500, and 720 − 500 = 220, there are 220 buns available at 3 pm.

7 The hundreds digit must be at least 6 and the ones digit must be odd. The numbers are 725, 745, 785, 825, 827, 845, 847, 857, 875. There are 9 numbers.

8 As B is in the middle of 0 and 2 it must represent 1. The number line is split into quarters. Halfway between 1 and 2 is $1\frac{1}{2}$. This means D represents $1\frac{1}{2}$.

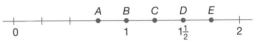

9 As $6 \times 4 = 24$, the value of X is 24. As $24 \div 3 = 8$, the value of Y is 8. As $24 − 8 = 16$, the difference is 16.

10 This shape is not possible.

11 As $6 \times 6 = 36$, there is a total of 36 faces of small squares on the shape. 4 faces can be seen from the front and another 4 faces from the back. 5 faces can be seen from the top and another 5 from the bottom. 4 faces can be seen from the side, and another 4 from the opposite side. As 4 + 4 + 5 + 5 + 4 + 4 = 26, and 36 − 26 = 10, there are 10 faces that cannot be seen.

12 As 50 − 20 = 30 and 30 ÷ 3 is 10, there are 10 numbers. These numbers are 21, 24, 27, 30, 33, 36, 39, 42, 45 and 48.

13 Look at the numbers in the top row and bottom row.
The rule is the bottom number = 2 × top number plus 3. Now 2 × 6 + 3 is 12 + 3 = 15, so the missing number is 15.

14 By counting, the perimeter of the rectangle is 10 of the square sides. As 20 ÷ 10 = 2, each square side has a length of 2 cm. As 2 × 2 = 4, each square has an area of 4 cm².

15 The smaller number is $\frac{1}{4}$ of 36 and the larger number is $\frac{3}{4}$ of 36. As 36 ÷ 4 = 9, the smaller number is 9. As 9 × 3 = 27, the larger number is 27. As 27 − 9 = 18, the difference between the two numbers is 18.

16 $P + 3 = 10$ means $P = 7$. Also, $5 + Q = 13$ which means $Q = 8$. The empty circles are $3 + 5 = 8$, and $8 + 13 = 21$.
This means $18 + 21 = R$, and so $R = 39$.
The sum of P, Q and R is $7 + 8 + 39 = 54$.
Here is the solved diagram:

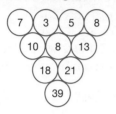

17 100, 90, 80, 70 is counting down by 10. The sequence continues: 100, 90, 80, 70, 60, 50, 40 …

18 As $9 - 8 = 1$, Byron can measure 1 cm. Also $5 - 3 = 2$, so 2 cm can be measured. And $8 - 5 = 3$, so 3 can be measured. Finally $9 - 5 = 4$ so 4 cm can be measured. But Byron cannot measure 7 cm accurately.

19 Shape X is a circle with 8 identical sectors. 5 out of the 8 sectors are shaded. This is $\frac{5}{8}$ of the shape, which is not the same as $\frac{3}{4}$. Shape Y is a square divided into 4 identical triangles. 3 out of the 4 triangles are shaded. This is $\frac{3}{4}$ of the shape. Shape Z is a rectangle split into 12 identical squares. 9 out of the 12 squares are shaded. This is $\frac{9}{12}$ of the rectangle, which is the same as $\frac{3}{4}$. This means Shapes Y and Z have $\frac{3}{4}$ shaded.

20 The scale shows the level of juice in Container Y is halfway between 600 and 900. This means 750 mL of juice is in Container Y. One-third of 300 is $300 \div 3 = 100$. As $750 + 100 = 850$, the container now has 850 mL of juice.

21 The number of cans used are 1, 3, 6 … These are triangular numbers. Adding 4 will give the next number of 10, adding 5 will give 15, and so on. Here are the first 7 numbers in the series: 1, 3, 6, 10, 15, 21, 28. Kyah will use 28 cans in Figure 7.

22 As 60×3 plus 5 is 185, the update will take 185 seconds. As $185 - 90 = 95$, there are 95 seconds remaining.

23 There are 2 lines of symmetry:

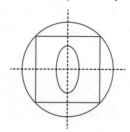

24 $23 + 11 = 34$ means that Milan is 34 days older than Alex. As 35 days is 5 weeks, the day before Milan's birthday is also a Sunday. This means Milan's birthday is on a Monday.

25 As G is south of A then it is directly under A on the grid. From A to G is 2 units, so the scale used is 2 units = 10 km, or 1 unit = 5 km. As $3 + 4 + 2 + 7 + 7 + 3 = 26$, the distance shown on the grid is 26 units. As $26 \times 5 = 130$, Greta's journey was 130 km.

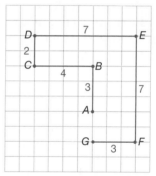

26 There are 2 rows of 4 identical squares which is 8 squares. There are 4 small squares in the middle of the shape. This means 12 squares have 4 right angles which is 48 right angles. But 4 of these right angles have already been counted. Also these small squares make 8 right angles when they overlap with the larger squares (shown on the diagram below). As $48 - 4 + 8 = 52$, there is a total of 52 right angles:

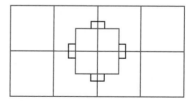

27 Two triangles are possible as well as two parallelograms. It is also possible to make a triangle and a pentagon, but not a hexagon:

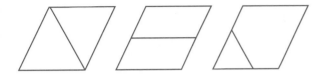

28 There is only one 6 out of 8 numbers. It is unlikely the arrow will stop on 6. Claim 1 is correct. There are 5 even numbers and 3 odd numbers. It is more likely that an even number is spun than an odd number. Claim 2 is not correct. There are two 4s and only one 8. It is more likely that the number 4 is spun than the number 8. Claim 3 is correct. Claims 1 and 3 are correct.

29 The first number is 48. As half of 48 plus 16 is 40, the second number is 40. As half of 40 plus 16 is 36, the third number is 36. As half of 36 plus 16 is 34, the fourth number is 34. As half of 34 plus 16 is 33, the fifth number is 33.

30 As 2 symbols represent 8 students, each symbol represents 4 students.
For cricket, 3 symbols = 12 students.
For netball, $1\frac{1}{2}$ symbols = 6 students.
As 12 − 6 = 6, there are 6 more students who prefer cricket to netball.

31 Four of the smaller shapes will fit into the larger shape.

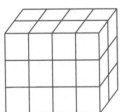

32 As 5 + 1 = 6, and 30 ÷ 6 = 5, the mass of the lighter crate is 5 kg. Crate *B* has a mass of 5 kg.

33 Mass of 6 balls = mass of 1 ball + 20 kg. This means the mass of 5 balls = 20 kg, and so each ball has a mass of 4 kg. This means 3 balls have a mass of 12 kg.

34 As 5 + 3 + 5 + 3 = 16, the perimeter of the rectangle is 16 units. As 16 × 2 = 32, the scale on the grid is 1 unit = 2 cm. This means the dimensions of the rectangle are 10 cm by 6 cm. As 10 × 6 = 60, the area is 60 cm².

35 More than 16 means 17, 18, 19 and 20.
Girls: 6 + 9 + 7 + 6 = 28.
Boys: 4 + 10 + 8 + 4 = 26.
As 28 − 26 = 2, there were 2 more girls than boys who scored more than 16.

THINKING SKILLS Test 1   Page 38

1 C	**2** B	**3** C	**4** B	**5** A	**6** C
7 C	**8** D	**9** D			
10 B	**11** D	**12** B	**13** C	**14** A	**15** D
16 B	**17** A	**18** B	**19** A	**20** B	**21** A
22 D	**23** A	**24** C	**25** C	**26** D	**27** B
28 D	**29** B	**30** A			

1 Questions like this are always easier once a diagram is drawn. Something as simple as a line with arrows for trains can help you see the way to the answer.

From the departure and arrival times of the first train, it took 3 hours to make the journey. If it took 3 hours for the first train, it must have taken 6 hours for the second train to make its journey, as it was travelling only half the speed of the first train. After the first 2 hours, the first train will have travelled two-thirds of the distance, and the second train will have travelled one-third of the distance.

Looking at the diagram below you can see that the trains will be at the same place after 2 hours. This is at 11 am.

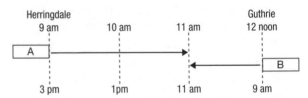

2 Taylor uses correct reasoning when he recognises that, because Adam does a lot of mountain biking, he is very fit. Taylor also allows room for doubt when he only says he thinks Adam will be fine. Elle makes a definite statement when she declares that Adam 'is going to hate it'. Even if she knows Adam really well, she cannot 'know' with any certainty what Adam is going to think about the hike.

3 This statement weakens the argument that China was the first country to make bronze coins. A and B strengthen the argument. D adds further information that neither strengthens nor weakens the argument.

4 The three movies I have chosen to see must be seen in Sessions 1, 2 and 3 as Session 4 does not contain *Toy Story 2* or *The Incredibles* and I can't see *Toy Story* then if I am to watch *Toy Story 2* after it. In the first three sessions I can watch *Toy Story* then *Toy Story 2* then *The Incredibles*, or *The Incredibles* then *Toy Story*, then *Toy Story 2*. This means I can see any of *Cars*, *Finding Nemo* or *Brave* in Session 4. I cannot see *Monsters Inc.* as it is only available in the first three sessions.

5 The main idea of Louella's text is that paleontologists are enthusiastically exploring for fossil remains of one of the largest mammals to roam the earth. The other sentences in the text describe the animal.

6 Priti is taller than Dylan and Mena, so she is the tallest.

7 Hari will perform during a period of 15 consecutive days which includes three Saturdays and two of every other day. To find the number of performances you can perform the calculation below: one for each day (15) + 1 extra for each Saturday (3) + 1 extra for each Thursday (2) – 1 for each Monday off (2):

$$15 + 3 + 2 - 2 = 18$$

8 Because every student had two votes, knowing that no student voted for both famous people as well as animals tells you that all students must have voted for book characters with one of their votes.

9 If Jack does not work then Naomi must be working. Since Naomi is working, Andrew must be working in place of Gemma. So Andrew and Naomi will work the next day.

10 If the square is on the top and the circle is on the left side, the hexagon would not be on the front right. Instead it would be on the back of the dice.

11 Only Bailey listed Karol and Anjali as friends.

12 The argument is that home-made ice cream tastes better because you can use exactly the ingredients you want. B is correct because this statement adds the concept of freshest ingredients and no preservatives. A supports the argument but not as much as B.

13 The following diagram shows the steps of the folding:

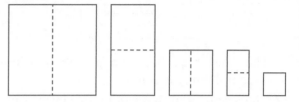

When unfolded, the piece of paper will have 16 small squares on it as shown below:

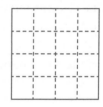

14 This statement best supports the argument that not eating nutritious foods leads to poor academic performance.

15 If Phil is sitting next to both Lana and Birender, then they are sitting in three consecutive seats around the table. That means the other three people are sitting in three consecutive seats. Chantelle can never be on the opposite side of the table to Miriam or David. The diagrams below show examples where Phil, Lana or Birender are opposite Chantelle:

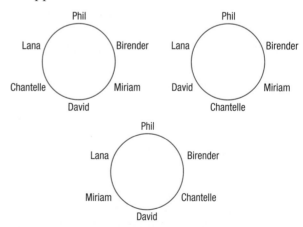

16 The only place this shape can go is shown below. This does not leave room for one of the other shapes to complete the square.

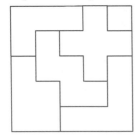

The other three shapes are all able to be used in completing the square.

17 The argument is that sustainable farms can coexist with native forests even though wildlife such as Sumatran tigers have lost habitat but if the tiger is endangered, it is not a good idea for it to lose any habitat at all. Therefore A weakens the argument.

18 The school won the sustainability award by planting indigenous vegetation so you can conclude that indigenous vegetation helps with sustainability. Other answers might be true but the information does not lead to those conclusions.

19 Graham's PB improves from 5.3 m to 6.9 m. This is an improvement of 1.6 m.

$$6.9 - 5.3 = 1.6$$

Using the same method we can see that Ashvin improved by 0.2 m, Johan improved by 1.5 m and Kyle improved by 0.9 m.

20 The information tells you that finishing work early and to an exceptional standard makes the teacher very happy with the class and, when she is happy with the class, she rewards the students with a games afternoon on the Friday. Other answers are incorrect because the reward of a games afternoon is given when the teacher is very happy with the class. Jed cannot conclude that last Friday's games afternoon was because of the class finishing work early and to a high standard. There might be another reason the teacher was happy with the class and rewarded them that week.

21 To be allowed to join the choir you have to attend the information session. Chester correctly reasons that he won't be able to join the choir because he can't attend the information session. Gabriella can attend the information session. This only means she will be allowed to audition for the choir; it does not mean she will get into the choir. Her reasoning is incorrect.

22 Every domino that has a five on it is shown below. There are seven.

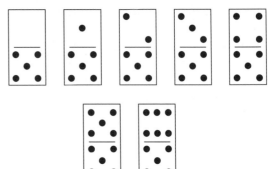

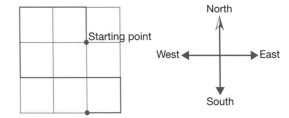

We can see from the string of dominoes in the question that four of these have been used already. That means there are three dominoes left in the set that can be used.

23 By tracing out his journey we can see that Angus ends up 200 m south of his starting point. That means he will have to travel 200 m north to return there:

The gridlines are 100 m apart.

24 Shantay has drawn the conclusion that Hetty likes putt-putt golf. Her evidence is that Hetty is organising putt-putt golf for her birthday. Her assumption is therefore that, if someone organises an activity for their birthday celebration, it will be something they enjoy doing.

25 By looking at the number of batches you can make with each ingredient, you will find that the carrots will be the ingredient that limits the number of batches that can be made.

9 sheets = 4.5 × 2 sheets

1 kg mince = 4 × 250 g

10 carrots = 2.5 × 4 carrots

6 eggs = 3 × 2 eggs

He has enough carrots to make 2.5 lots of the recipe exactly, which will produce 2.5 × 16 = 40 sausage rolls. There is more than enough of the other ingredients for this.

26 Chloe's conclusion is that Farid's family must be cooking up mountains of delicious food in preparation for the huge family gathering. Her evidence to reach this conclusion is that Farid's family is having a huge family gathering to meet the new baby. She is assuming that Farid's family has delicious food at huge family gatherings.

27 We start with one white and two blue faces.

If we turn the two blue cards over, then we end up with three white cards.

If instead we turn over a white and a blue, we end up with two blue and one white.

In either case, any turn after that can never produce three blue cards.

It can be seen that if we start with an odd number of white cards, there will always be an odd number of white cards and if we start with an even number of blue cards we will always have an even number of blue cards.

We can see that B has an odd number of blue cards, which is impossible. The other options are all possible.

28 There are three rooms, one of which is in the shape of a rectangle. This rules out B and C as B has no rectangles and C has two. The width of the room that has the long thin section is the point of difference between the other two floor plans. In the original diagram the width of this room means it doesn't come all the way to the top of the rectangular room. In A it takes it further than this. The answer therefore must be D.

29 If the white box is on the far left and there is only one box between it and the green box then the green box is in the middle of the row. If the black box is next to the orange box they must occupy the two spots furthest right, leaving the red box to occupy the spot second from the left. If the red box is next to the box with the present, and there is a box between it and the orange box, then the present must be in the green box.

| White | Red | ☆ Green | Black | Orange |

30 The text argues that Roald Dahl is one of the most popular children's authors in the world. The other statements in the argument include examples of Dahl's books and explain why they are popular.

THINKING SKILLS Test 2

Page 46

1 B 2 B 3 C 4 B 5 D 6 D 7 A 8 C 9 A
10 C 11 A 12 D 13 A 14 A 15 B 16 B
17 B 18 A 19 D 20 C 21 C 22 C 23 D
24 B 25 A 26 C 27 D 28 A 29 C 30 D

1 Questions like this are always easier once a diagram is drawn. Something as simple as a line with arrows for trains can help you see the way to the answer.

The train on the coast line will take exactly 1.5 times as long as the inland train to make the journey. The train on the coast line takes 5 h to make the trip. It is easier to see the answer if the 5 h are converted into 300 min.

The train travelling along the coast line takes 300 min:

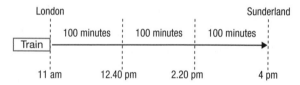

The train travelling inland takes 200 min:

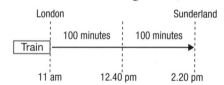

We can see that 300 min is 1.5 times the length of 200 min. So the train arrived at 2:20 pm.

2 This statement best supports doctors' claims because it reinforces the need for the recommended safety harness in order to prevent injuries.

3 The argument is that it's easy to grow tomatoes at home. The statement that there are numerous common problems encountered by people growing tomatoes at home weakens the argument that it is easy.

4 Rock climbing is only available in Session 2 so I must do it then. Orienteering is now only available in Session 3 so I must do it then. The only activity of mine in Session 4 is High ropes, so I must do that then. This means that in Session 1 I must do the Assault course.

5 Triple trouble luxe was more popular than Magic mountain mint, which was more popular than Rolling in the dough. Rolling in the dough was preferred over Gingerbread swirl and Three berry ripple. So the most popular flavour was Triple trouble luxe.

6 From the information Tim must be the furthest to the left. So the other three can only be on the end if they are furthest to the right. Connor is always to the left of Kylie so he cannot ever be furthest to the right.

The two possible orders from left to right are:

- Tim, Connor, Kylie then Jules
- Tim, Jules, Connor then Kylie.

7 There are 61 days from 1 March to 1 May. Similarly there are 61 days from 3 March to 3 May and therefore 62 days from 3 March to 4 May.

If we start on a Monday, after seven days we get back to a Monday. Each lot of seven days leaves us at the same day of the week, so we can take away groups of seven to make the question easier.

$$62 - 8 \times 7 = 62 - 56$$
$$= 6$$

So 4 May will be six days after a Monday. It lands on a Sunday.

8 Based on the information in the box, both people are correct. Pandora correctly reasons that the owners of the dog in unit 8, whose barking interferes with neighbours' use and enjoyment of their units because it barks all day, will probably be notified that it cannot live in the building if its behaviour continues. Tristan correctly reasons that the owners' corporation would need to prove that the dog's behaviour was continually interfering with other residents' enjoyment of their units otherwise the Owners' Corporation would be acting unreasonably.

9 Because Hikaru has ordered a new printer, Elisabeth has concluded that the old printer is to be recycled (thrown out). In order to draw this conclusion, Elisabeth must have assumed the old printer is broken. If the printer was still working, it could be sold or given away. The fact she wants to dispose of it tells you she thinks it must be broken.

10 If the hexagon is on the top and the circle is on the left side, the square would not be on the front right. Instead it would be on the back right of the dice, exactly opposite the circle.

11 The main idea of the paragraph is that sustainable insect farming benefits the environment. Three reasons are given in the paragraph to support the argument: saving forests, reducing methane gasses and saving water use.

12 This conclusion is not possible. From the information in the box, you can draw the conclusion that if the bike is not cleaned and in good working order it won't sell for a good price.

13 If a note goes up one octave when the string is halved in length, it will go down one octave if the string is doubled in length. So we need to find out how many times 3 cm is doubled to get to 24 cm.

$$3 \times 2 \times 2 \times 2 = 24$$

The string is doubled in length three times, which means the note will be 3 octaves lower.

14 The information in the box tells you **almost** every kind of monkey has a tail. Sana is incorrect when she says that if it's a non-human primate and it doesn't have a tail, it has to be an ape.

15 If Isaac is sitting diagonally opposite Rene then they are sitting on the long sides of the table. If Rene is sitting opposite Carl, then Carl must be sitting on the long side of the table, next to Isaac. If Pierre and Emmy sit next to each other, they occupy the two empty seats next to each other. If Ada and Emmy are sitting opposite each other then they are at the ends and Pierre must be sitting next to Rene. Following is one of the arrangements possible:

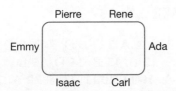

Ada will always be between Rene and Carl.

16 Option B cannot be used as it never leaves enough space to fit any of the other shapes without leaving gaps:

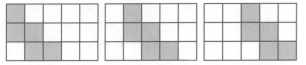

The other three shapes can be arranged like so:

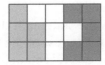

17 The claim is that only produce grown at home is heathier than produce sold at the market. Produce grown without pesticides might be heathier than produce grown with pesticides so B weakens the claim. D would weaken a claim that the markets are a convenient way to shop for produce but does not weaken a claim about the healthiness of the produce.

18 The argument wants you to accept that we should go out and experience the dark more often and A is the statement that best expresses this. The rest of the argument gives you reasons to believe this main idea, with supporting details about why and how we should experience the dark.

19 Ramesh's conclusion is that Lola must not lose her hat. For it to hold, it must be assumed that Lola should not do something that would upset her mum: if Lola loses another hat, her mum will get upset + Lola should not do something that would upset her mum = therefore Lola must not lose the hat.

20 Of those who improved their ranking, Tess went from 2nd to 1st, Lauren went from 4th to 3rd, Ezi went from 6th to 4th, and Nneka went from 8th to 7th. Ezi improved her rank among her teammates by two positions, whereas the other players only improved by one.

21 According to the instructor, if a scuba diver has not completed open-water dives then they do not have a chance of being certified. Therefore none of the scuba divers who have not completed open-water dives will be certified.

22 The space at the bottom of the square cannot have a domino with a six on it. Both 2 and 4 have a six on them so there is no way that either will fit that space while still following the rule. All the other options are possible.

23 The region looks like this:

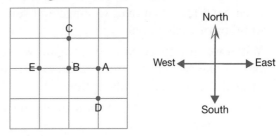

We can see that Town E is south-west of Town C.

The other options are not correct as Town E and Town B are 10 km apart, Town C is north-west of Town A and Town D is south-east of Town B.

24 We know Dylan's dad always sings old songs when he's in a good mood and he's always in a good mood when he wins a race. So Zara's reasoning is correct. However, there might also be other reasons why he's in a good mood. Therefore Dylan's reasoning is incorrect.

25 The tennis balls sold in the 10-pack are $2.50 each, as $25 ÷ 10 = $2.50.

The tennis balls sold in the 4-pack are $2.75 each, as $11 ÷ 4 = $2.75.

The tennis balls sold in the 3-pack are $3 each, as $9 ÷ 3 = $3.

The individual balls are $4.

This means that the more balls Jillian can buy in the 10-pack, the more balls she can buy. She should then look to buy balls in a 4-pack as they are the next cheapest, and so on.

A 10-pack and a 4-pack and a single ball together cost exactly $40. 25 + 11 + 4 = 40

This gets Jillian 10 + 4 + 1 = 15 balls.

26 This option provides the best reason to support the politician's claim that the tunnel will benefit the local community.

27 We start with two white and two blue faces.

When we turn three cards over, we either turn two white cards and one blue or we turn two blue cards and one white. This leaves us with three of one colour and one of the other. So after one move we have an odd number of each colour.

When we turn three cards over again, we either get four of one colour or we get two of each. So after two moves we have an even number of each colour.

When we turn three cards over again we get one of one colour and three of the other. So after three turns, the only option is D.

This pattern will continue for as many moves as we make.

28 The building has only three rooms. This rules out C. Only one of the rooms is a rectangle. This rules out D as it has two rectangular rooms. The middle room is not the rectangular room. This rules out B. The answer is A.

29 First we put Carlos in the house furthest to the right. Alexis is not in the house next door to this so must be in one of the first three houses. If he is also three doors away from Emily, the only way this works is if he is in the first house and Emily lives next to Carlos. Dave lives two doors from Emily so must be in the second house on the left leaving Bella to live in the third house from the left;

Alexis	Dave	Bella	Emily	Carlos

30 Mr Flint has concluded that some of the children must have forgotten their library books because he knows 15 children have books due and he only saw eight children carrying library bags. Therefore he must think that children always bring their library books in a library bag. However, some children might have brought their books in a different bag.

THINKING SKILLS Test 3 Page 54

1 C	2 B	3 D	4 A	5 C	6 D	7 D	8 C	9 A
10 B	11 C	12 B	13 B	14 D	15 D	16 B
17 A	18 A	19 D	20 D	21 C	22 A	23 C
24 B	25 B	26 D	27 D	28 C	29 B	30 A

1 The Ferrari can finish 10 laps in 30 min. Doing this twice means it would do 20 laps in 60 min.

The Porsche can complete 15 laps in 30 min, which is 5 laps every 10 min. This means it will complete the 20 laps in 40 min total.

The Porsche will beat the Ferrari by the difference in the times: $60 - 40 = 20$ min.

2 The text wants you to accept that human bodies are designed to breathe in through the nose and B is the statement that best expresses this. The rest of the text gives you reasons to believe this main idea, with supporting details about different benefits of breathing in through the nose instead of the mouth.

3 The instructor says anyone who does not understand person overboard recovery does not have a chance of passing the course. So there cannot be any students who do not understand person overboard recovery who will pass the course.

4 Ceramics, Textiles and Lino printing must be chosen from Lists 1, 3 and 4 as none of those courses are available in List 2. This means only the courses in List 2 can be chosen as the last course. Animation is not available in List 2 (only in Lists 3 and 4) so cannot be chosen. Animation is the correct answer.

Sketching, Portraiture and Working with wood are in List 2 so can be chosen and are not the answer.

5 Monti has assumed that students only do projects about topics they know a lot about. However, students could also choose a topic they are not so familiar with and do some research.

6 Both the Screensource and the Tellysonic are more expensive than the Visionary, so the Visionary must be the least expensive. The other three options are all possible but not necessarily true.

7   15th, 22nd and 29th are all Thursdays so there are two full weeks from 15th to 28th, then three extra days Thursday 29th, Friday 30th and Saturday 31st.

In each full week there are 8 performances (1 each for Monday, Wednesday, Thursday and Friday and four on the weekend).

So there is a total of 2 × 8 (for the two full weeks) plus 4 for the extra Thursday, Friday and Saturday. This is a total of 20 less the one day Xander was injured. So Xander performed 19 times.

8   This option provides the best reason to support the tour company's claim that the weekend forest package is good for people's health.

9   We can see on the net that if the square is connected to the top of the triangle, the pentagon will be on the right of the triangle. But the view of the dice in the question shows the pentagon clearly on the left.

10 We are told that only customers with over 100 points will be allowed to buy the model but this does not mean all those customers will **definitely** buy the model. Therefore Blake's reasoning is incorrect. Evie does not have enough points to be allowed to buy the model so Mia's reasoning is correct.

11 Having an allergy to a pet would not be good for a person's wellbeing so this statement weakens the doctor's claim. All the other statements support the claim.

12 If Ria does not have leftovers, she will have pizza. And since she has pizza, she must also have salad.

13 Looking at the diagrams below you can see what the final small triangle will look like.

The long side of this triangle is half the width of the original square. So the original square is twice this length.

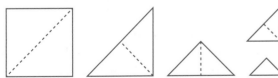

14 Joe's conclusion is that Uma must love playing netball. For it to hold, it must be assumed that anyone who plays netball every Saturday must love playing netball: Uma plays netball every Saturday + anyone who plays netball every Saturday loves playing netball = therefore Uma must love playing netball.)

15 If John is sitting with his back to the window and George is sitting next to Ringo, it is impossible for Paul to be sitting opposite John. He therefore cannot be facing the window:

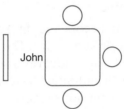

16 We cannot use the shape in Option B to cover the grid. You can see by the diagram below that there will always be overlap and corners missing:

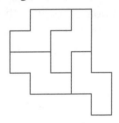

The solutions for the others are:

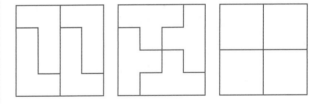

17 This option provides the best reason to support Tony's claim that live television is better than streaming because live television is more exciting.

18 We know that only musicians who have attended every band practice this term will be allowed to go to the concert. So, since Quan missed a practice, he will not be allowed to go and his reasoning is correct. Aziz's reasoning is incorrect because, even though he attended every band practice, there may be other reasons why some musicians are unable to go so it is a flaw in his reasoning to say he will **definitely** be allowed to go.

19 The difference between the original and sale prices will give the amount saved:

For the Mowfast: $729 - 599 = 130$

For the Blades-begone: $379 - 199 = 180$

For the First Cut: $1060 - 899 = 161$

For the Victory: $799 - 609 = 190$

Buying the Victory will save him $190 on the original price. This is a bigger saving than on any of the others.

20 Bridge and periscope are on Arlo's list but not on Lucy or Suma's list. The other options are incorrect: rope ladder is also on Suma's list; both Lucy and Suma have slippery dip on their list; and neither swing nor zipline are on Arlo's list.

21 The sales assistant has found a skateboard that matches the description from Bree's mother and assumes it **must** be the one Sophie wants. However, it might not be the correct skateboard because there might be other designs that are green with a shark.

22 If we look at all dominoes that have a blank square, there are seven dominoes and eight blank squares.

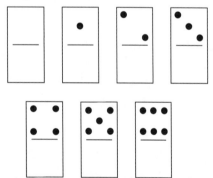

We can say the same for each number. Each number appears eight times over seven dominoes. If each number (including the blank) appears eight times there are $8 \times 7 = 56$ squares used. As each domino has two squares there are $56 \div 2 = 28$ dominoes.

Another way of finding the answer is to work through each number. There are seven dominoes with blanks. Seeing as one of those has a one on it, there are only six dominoes left with ones on them. Now, we already have two dominoes with a two on them, so there are five left.

This continues until we have only the double-six to count in the sixes as all the other dominoes with six on them have been counted already.

$$7 + 6 + 5 + 4 + 3 + 2 + 1 = 28$$

23 It is often best to approach questions like this by looking to rule out options as you read through the information in the question.

The first piece of information does not rule any options out as Town A is always more north than Town C.

The second piece of information rules out options A and D as Town C is the southernmost town yet needs to be more north than Town D.

The last piece of information rules out option B as Town B is the westernmost town but needs to be more east than town E.

This leaves our answer as C.

24 This option provides the best reason to support the architect's claim that the building should be turned into a space for film and music.

25 By looking at the number of batches that can be made with each ingredient, we find that the butter will be the ingredient that limits the number of batches that can be made.

375g of butter will allow him to bake three batches as $375 \text{ g} = 3 \times 125 \text{ g}$.

He has enough of everything else to make three batches but cannot make any more than that. Three batches will use 540 g of sugar as $3 \times 180 \text{ g} = 540 \text{ g}$. If he starts with 1 kg of sugar he will have 460 g left over as $1000 \text{ g} - 540 \text{ g} = 460 \text{ g}$.

26 Since everyone had to vote for two out of the three ideas, knowing that no student voted for both computer corner and science centre tells you all students must have voted for reading corner. Reading corner must also have been the only idea all students voted for because each idea got at least one vote.

27 If he dropped a green and a red ball he would have three differently coloured balls left in his hands. He only has two colours left so this is not possible.

28 The building has three rooms. This rules out A. There is only one rectangular room and it is the middle one. This rules out B and D. The answer is C.

29 If we number the cups from left to right we can follow them a little more easily.

Number 1 moves to the far right. Number 2 and 3 must be separated by two cups, which means they are in positions 1 and 4. If the ball is not in the middle cup it must be in the second cup from the left, and the row would look like this:

30 Locky has concluded that, since he practises for the required amount of time, he will **definitely** pass the exam. However, just because everybody who passes the exam practises for at least that amount of time, it does not mean everybody who practises for that amount of time will pass the exam.

NOTES

NOTES

NOTES